The Women of Genesis

The Women of Genesis

From Sarah to Potiphar's Wife

Sharon Pace Jeansonne

Fortress Press

Minneapolis

THE WOMEN OF GENESIS
From Sarah to Potiphar's Wife

Scripture quotations are translated directly from the original language by the author. Some scripture quotations are from the Revised Standard Version of the Bible, copyright © 1946, 1952, and 1971 by the Division of Christian Education of the National Council of Churches.

Cover art: "The Meeting of Jacob and Rachel" by Marc Chagall. Copyright © Haggerty Museum of Art, Marquette University, Milwaukee, Wisconsin. All rights reserved. Used by permission.

Library of Congress Cataloging-in-Publication Data
Jeansonne, Sharon Pace 1956-
    The women of Genesis : from Sarah to Potiphar's wife / Sharon Pace
Jeansonne.
        p.   cm.
    ISBN 0-8006-2419-X
    1. Bible. O.T. Genesis—Criticism, interpretation. etc.
    2. Women in the Bible.   3. Woman (Theology)—Biblical teaching.
    I. Title.
    BS1235.6.W7J43   1990
    221'.110922'082—dc20   89-78124
                                                                        CIP

The paper used in this publication meets the minimum requirements of American National Standard for Information Sciences—Permanence of Paper for Printed Library Materials, ANSI Z329.48-1984.   ∞™

Manufactured in the U.S.A.   AF 1-2419

00   99   98   4   5   6   7   8   9   10   11   12

To Glen

Contents

Preface

The current generation of biblical interpreters increasingly recognizes that past studies of women in the Bible have suffered from patriarchal bias. Simplistic stereotypes of female characters and their reduction to minor significance have prompted many biblical scholars to reconsider the texts in a new perspective. Because of its placement as the first book of the Bible, Genesis has held a particularly noteworthy place in interpreting the history, sociology, and theology of the Israelite community. The women featured in the Genesis narratives play crucial roles in the developing story line of Israel's origins.

Rather than investigate the texts for their historical or sociological import, I have undertaken a narrative-critical approach that examines the functions the women perform in enhancing our understanding of the Book of Genesis as story and art. I have begun the investigation at Genesis 12, the narrative that begins to unfold Israel's self-understanding as a people who originate with Abraham and Sarah. I investigate individual narratives as they currently stand in Genesis and I consider their literary features and relationships to the greater narrative context. My premise is that the content and arrangement of narratives in Genesis is crafted literary art.

While some modern interpreters claim that the patriarchal structures from which the stories come make them hopelessly inappropriate for today, I feel that the stories often were poignant and inspiring for the audience who originally heard them, and still have relevance for us who seek to learn not only what the text meant but what it can mean.

I am indebted to the many people who contributed to the formation of this book. Pamela Milne of the University of Windsor kindly read the manuscript and offered insights. My colleagues John Schmitt and Rita Burns of Marquette University carefully critiqued the study. One chapter was presented to the theology faculty colloquium, and I profited from questions raised there and from written suggestions given by Julian Hills. The chair of the theology department, Phillip Rossi, assisted me in obtaining research support and furnished leave time. Carol Stockhausen encouraged me to apply for the Catholic Biblical Association's fellowship, and I wish to thank the CBA for granting me the Young Scholar Award for 1987–88. Marquette University's Office of Research Support aided my writing with a Summer Faculty Fellowship in 1988 and the theology department provided me a Released Time Award in fall 1988 to complete the manuscript. My research assistant, John Grabowski, was an excellent proofreader and checked numerous references. I wish to thank Lyndall Bass and Glenna Jackson for their help. The rabbis at my synagogue, Jay Brickman and Terry Bookman, offered many insights into the texts, as did my friends and professional writers Charlotte Gallagher and Amy Waldman. I am particularly grateful to Charlotte Gallagher, who patiently edited drafts of each chapter and offered encouragement throughout the writing of the book. The study was improved by the questions and suggestions of John A. Hollar of Fortress Press, whose untimely death in October of 1989 greatly saddened me. Stefanie Ormsby Cox of Fortress Press was most helpful in preparing the final stages of the manuscript. Jane ten Brink Goldsmith of Marquette University's Haggerty Museum kindly provided the Chagall print, which is reproduced on the cover. My dear husband, Glen Jeansonne, frequently set aside his own research in order to read drafts of the manuscript. In the course of writing this book we had our first child, Leah. My joy and delight in our daughter have brought me a new awareness of the significance of the stories in Genesis.

Abbreviations

Ant.	*Antiquities*
BASOR	*Bulletin of the American Schools of Oriental Research*
BHS	*Biblia Hebraica Stuttgartensia*
BR	*Biblical Research*
BTB	*Biblical Theology Bulletin*
CBQ	*Catholic Biblical Quarterly*
Gen. Rab.	*Genesis Rabbah*
HrvTR	*Harvard Theological Review*
JBL	*Journal of Biblical Literature*
JJS	*Journal of Jewish Studies*
JSOT	*Journal for the Study of the Old Testament*
JSOTS	Journal for the Study of the Old Testament Supplement Series
RB	Revue biblique
RSV	Revised Standard Version
SBL	Society of Biblical Literature
VT	*Vetus Testamentum*

1

Introduction

Until recently most modern interpreters of the Book of Genesis have displayed patriarchal bias. Their commentaries consider women chiefly in their function of supporting men, and the portraits of women's lives are not seriously examined for their inherent significance. Texts concerning women are often misunderstood or ignored. For example, Sarah's laughter at God's promise that she will bear a child is interpreted as an example of her moral failure, yet Abraham's laughter is seen to be justified. Lot offers to have his daughters raped by all the men of the city in order to spare the divine messengers, who are clearly capable of defending themselves, from this threatened fate. The vast majority of commentators still judge Lot as a righteous character while they dismiss the threatened sexual abuse of his daughters as "oriental hospitality." This portrayal is maintained despite literary evidence that reveals Lot as a self-serving individual. Rebekah, Rachel, and Leah are considered only in relation to their husbands, Isaac and Jacob, despite the presence of texts where these women appear without men. For example, God reveals information to Rebekah that is vital for the fulfillment of the promise of descendants. Leah and Rachel are responsible for the inauguration of the tribes and arrange for their families' safe return to Canaan. The horror of Dinah's rape and her brothers' subsequent acts of revenge are not considered from the victim's perspective even though the narrator shows that this is a crucial concern.

This absence of recognition combined with biased interpretations has led to a misunderstanding of the Book of Genesis. Because women feature prominently in this first book of the Bible, any attempt to understand the historical, narrative, or theological perspective fairly must incorporate the narratives that feature them. Since the advent of feminist hermeneutics, such biased interpretations have been increasingly challenged. Interest has increased in biblical texts that deal with women, using various approaches to investigate these texts.[1] Some studies attempt to discover challenges to patriarchy while others examine and critique structures that allocated to women specified roles. Such studies no longer are limited to academic journals. They now reach broader audiences, incorporating the scholarly gains in this new understanding of biblical narrative and Israelite history.[2]

Many crucial aspects of the theology of the Israelite community are strategically placed in the Book of Genesis. In fact, Genesis deservedly is one of the most studied books in the Hebrew Bible. My study will focus upon the ancestral narratives that describe the self-understanding of the origins of the Israelite people in Genesis 12–50. Understanding the relevance of the women within the ancestral history of Israel will provide a clearer assessment of the narrative emphasis of these texts. Far from using women as ancillary props, the narrator depicts them as persons who undergird Israel's origins. These accounts reveal perspectives on God's involvement with the Israelites as well as portrayals of human freedom, strength, and failure. God as the giver of fertility and the sustainer of the promise of blessing is unequivocally demonstrated through the lives of Israel's foremothers.

God's designs for the nation of Israel and for other peoples are revealed to Hagar and Rebekah. Personal portraits are equally important. Sarah and Rebekah, at risk when they travel to foreign lands because their husbands do not acknowledge them as wives, remain independent women who determine the destiny of their people. Sarah and Rachel, who must wait an inordinate period of time before they have children, inflict pain upon those who are forced to share in their hardships. They help demonstrate that Israel's interconnectedness with foreign peoples is extraordinarily complex. Hagar and Leah, who suffer in their role as the least favored wife, shift their focus from their tormentors to their children, who are considered gifts from God. Hagar is mistreated and brought to the threshold of death; the daughters of Lot are threatened with rape by all the men of their city; Dinah is raped by Shechem and mistreated by her brothers; and Tamar is abandoned and denied her marital rights. Yet, in the face of adversity, these women demonstrate great resilience and resourcefulness. Rebekah helps implement one of God's covenantal promises. Hagar moves from slave to independent woman. Tamar is vindicated when she obtains children from Judah, who acknowledges the injustice he has inflicted on her. Although Dinah's pain

2

never is alleviated, the narrator uses her story to condemn the violence and estrangement between the Israelites and Shechemites.

Method: Preliminary Remarks

Biblical scholarship in the last two decades has produced studies of the oral origins of texts, the literary forms they take, the events that prompt them, their changes over the course of their literary tradition, and their parallels in the literature of the ancient Near East. Typically, interpreters have identified and analyzed the numerous traditions that contributed to the text in its final version and have written voluminously on the minutiae of the Hebrew Scriptures.

An increasing number of biblical interpreters, however, have identified the weaknesses in these approaches. Although they have been helpful in understanding the individual parts and identifying the background from which texts develop, these traditional methods have not examined texts as they presently stand in relationship to the greater narrative context. They have failed to recognize the subtle, multiple ways in which the narrator uses one text to comment on another (intertexuality) or to develop the overall themes of an entire book.

Narrative criticism, the method employed in this book, addresses such concerns. Narrative critics analyze the particular literary features that the narrator uses to develop not only an individual narrative, but also to deliberately link it with other stories in the larger context for a distinctive design. Throughout this study, individual scenes that deal with each woman are examined in the context of the entirety of references to her and to the events that pertain to her story. Sometimes the women in Genesis are portrayed in ways that stress their equality and importance, but in other instances their portraits are oversimplifications. Questions to consider are: What is the narrator's view of the person being described and the characters who interact with her? How does the plot develop? How rapidly does the narrative proceed? How is dialogue used and to what purpose? What is God's relationship to the woman? How does the woman's life affect the promises of land, descendants, and blessing? While the approach is narrative-critical, past historical-critical work is not neglected, and the reader will find several references to the important results of other methodologies.

Now I want to describe some of the representative narrative features contained in the investigations of the following chapters.

Characterization and Dialogue

Details of an individual's personality are provided by description of action, commentary, and dialogue. The actions of individuals not only move the plot forward, but enable the reader to form judgments about characterization. Pharaoh gives gifts to Abraham and Sarah even after he discovers that they have wrongfully deceived him; the narrator thereby contrasts his generous behavior with the failure of Abraham to act fairly. Lot's dispute with Abraham over division of the land yields the first glimpses of his self-serving nature and places his indifference toward his daughters in context. Moreover, when told by the angel to act to save his family, he instead merely speaks to his sons-in-law. Thus he proves his repeated inability to obey divine directions. Hagar demonstrates her strength and independence by selecting a wife for her son from among her own people, a task usually undertaken by the father. Rebekah appears strong and determined when she encounters Abraham's servant, both by taking the initiative to provide for his needs and by making a commitment to leave her family. The narrator thus foreshadows the role she will play by helping to determine God's choice of Jacob as the covenantal heir. Laban initially appears generous when offering hospitality to Abraham's servant, but there are clues that he is motivated by the gifts bestowed on his sister. Later, his selfish character is demonstrated unequivocally in his relations with his daughters and with Jacob. Isaac not only appears foolish when he endangers Rebekah by having her claim to be his sister, but also when he fondles her openly, thereby revealing that she is his wife.

Examples of the narrator's direct commentary on an individual's character or upon events include the descriptions of Jacob as a reflective youth and that of Esau as a man of the field. These comments prepare the reader for Rebekah's favoritism toward Jacob, who appears more worthy to be the heir to the covenantal promises than does Esau, whose marriages to foreign women and cavalier sale of his birthright are consonant with the description of his personality. When Sarah dares to laugh at God's message that she will have a child, the narrator reveals that she does so only because she is afraid, thereby permitting the reader to understand and sympathize with her. Far from yielding superfluous details, characterization yields insight into the narrative itself.

Dialogue is another important means used in a writer's characterization. Insights into an individual's treatment of another person, his or her own growth or development, and understanding of God may be revealed in his or her speech.[3] The point at which a person speaks, as well as the content and formulation, is indicative of his or her ideas, status, role, and power. Abraham's conversation with Pharaoh reveals his own lack of understanding of God's providential care for him and his weak excuse for endangering his wife, whereas Pharaoh's true understanding of the God of Abraham stands in marked contrast. Rebekah at first seems powerless in the controversy over the time of her departure. When she does speak, however, it is with determinative judgment. Her conversation with Jacob, in which she details her plan for him to receive Isaac's blessing, demonstrates her authoritative stance. The dialogue between Rachel and Leah concerning the use of mandrakes as an aphrodisiac serves as a powerful reminder of Leah's pain because Jacob does not love her, and as a reminder of Rachel's anguish over her childlessness. Furthermore, the women's ability to determine Jacob's sexual partner on any given occasion is also demonstrated. In addition, their unity in answering Jacob's request to leave their father shows that they have the courage to act together and thus avoid a further injustice from their father. Tamar's forthright dialogue with Judah about his payment for having sex with her shows her to have the upper hand and underscores his ignorance.

Perspective and Authority

The narrator writes from a position of privileged perspective. The narrator is privy to the thoughts and feelings of the characters; moreover, the narrator knows God's perspective. Thus, the narrator speaks from an omniscient view, having access to the past and future as well as to present events.[4] Information may be given from a variety of perspectives: that of a character, the narrator, or God.

Information from the character's perspective enables the reader to have a sense of his or her feelings and motivation, or provides information on how to assess the person's particular performance or activity. For example, Lot addresses the angels of God as men and seems blind to their true identity, which underscores his own weakness in perception. By presenting this information from Lot's perspective the narrator's own negative judgment of Lot appears less dominant, enabling the reader to reach his or her own conclusion. The anguish of Lot's daughters is revealed by their own words when they conclude that there are no men left on earth with whom to have children, allowing the reader to understand why they committed incest with their own father. Jacob laments that his people are few in number and cannot withstand the turmoil that his sons have instigated against the Shechemites. Because the fear of the consequences emanates from the leader of the nascent Israelite people himself, the narrator thus emphasizes the magnitude of the sons' crime.

The narrator's own reflective comments are also given, thereby providing a less ambiguous clue for understanding the narrator's interpretation. When Abraham suggests that he and Lot divide the land to keep the peace, Lot chooses the best portion, leaving the reader with no doubts that Lot was selfish and uncompromising. If there were any question that perhaps Lot was spared because he was one of the ten righteous men of Sodom, the narrator states that Lot was rescued because of God's mercy and because God remembered Abraham. The narrator reveals that Esau's marriages were very troublesome to both Isaac and Rebekah, equating foreign marriages with the rejection of the community's ways. Jacob's seven years of labor for Rachel seemed but a few days to him, leaving no doubt as to the intensity of his love. Sometimes the narrator reveals an individual's emotions through an omniscient viewpoint because the character's own words might lack credibility. The threat of Ishmael to Isaac is shown through the narrator's description of Sarah's fearful perspective rather than through her direct words so that the reader can understand her harsh treatment of her servant. Similarly, the narrator informs the reader that Shechem came to love Dinah rather than using the words of her rapist, which would be suspect.

The narrator in Genesis may present unquestionable viewpoints or clarifications by giving information from God's perspective. This can be done by direct or indirect discourse. For example, the poignancy of Leah's plight is unquestionable because God "saw that Leah was hated" (29:31 RSV),[5] and thus responds to her by giving her children. The angel of God speaks directly to Hagar saying that God "has heard about your suffering" (16:11), underscoring God's intervention in the conflict between her and Sarah. If there were any question as to whether Abimelech approached Sarah sexually, the narrator clarifies by quoting God's direct speech to Abimelech indicating that God did not allow him to touch her.

Ambiguity and Gaps

The narrator may withhold information in order to encourage the reader to consider all sides when the merits of events or activity must be adjudicated, to heighten suspense, to present a more powerful characterization, or to underscore God's designs in the lives of the individuals. This absence of information may occur in the narrator's delineation of events, description of details, or in the presentation of characterization.[6]

6

Ambiguity concerning what occurred may be seen in the narrative of Sarah and Abraham's encounter with Pharaoh. The narrator never explicitly states nor denies that Sarah has a sexual relationship with Pharaoh. Pharaoh states that he "took her to me as a wife" (12:19) instead of the more explicit "I went into her." Thus, the potential of the threat and danger to Sarah looms prominently, yet Sarah's faithfulness to Abraham is never compromised.

Ambiguity in details also provokes the reader to consider more than one possibility of interpretation. For example, Hagar is identified as the *šipḥāh* (maidservant) of Sarah, the same term used of the servants Abraham obtained in Egypt. The narrator thus suggests that Sarah's difficulties with Hagar may have their roots in Abraham's earlier scheme but never resolves the question. When Rachel steals her father's idols, Jacob unwittingly proclaims the death sentence on her as punishment. Fortunately, her claim that she is menstruating saves her from Laban's search. The narrator fails to indicate whether or not Rachel actually has her period and withholds the dramatic conclusion by describing the details of the search. This highlights Rachel's cleverness as well as the drama of the account.

The complexity of characterization may be developed also by ambiguity. When Sarah again encounters a foreign ruler, Abraham defends his deception to Abimelech by stating that Sarah is in fact his half-sister. However, the narrator never confirms her genealogy, thus leaving open the possibility that Abraham is lying. When Dinah is raped, Jacob's response is never given, yielding at least two possibilities of interpretation. Does he care for her welfare? Or is he acting with restraint in order to avert an even greater disaster? Indeed, the question of revenge versus honor is important in this narrative. The narrator saves for the very end of the account Judah's recognition that his treatment of Tamar was wrong. This underscores his maltreatment of her as well as his moral blindness.

Theological themes, such as the implications of God's promises and God's role in the people's continuing existence, are developed also by withholding information. When Sarah tells Abraham to dismiss Hagar and Ishmael, the narrator states that the matter disturbs Abraham "on account of his son" (21:11 RSV). By not specifying whether the son is Ishmael or Isaac, both the dismissal of Ishmael and his genuine threat to Isaac are appropriately kept in tension. The reader is not told that Rachel will indeed bear Jacob a son until after her long struggle is over in order that God's role as the giver of fertility can be unequivocally expressed. Although Joseph's life is endangered by the lies of Potiphar's wife and Joseph is imprisoned by Potiphar himself, Joseph marries Asenath, who is identified as the daughter of Potiphara, priest of On. The narrator never specifies whether Potiphar is Potiphara, but by raising the possibility encourages the reader to consider the often surprising nature of God's providence.

Repetition

Repetitions of dialogue, of particular words, or of descriptions are devices that can reveal much about the veracity of the speaker's words, the integrity of his or her motives, the purpose of God's designs, or the development of the narrative itself. Repetition is never simply retelling. It demonstrates the crucial aspects of events or scenes that remain the same and the significant variations of the narrative elements.[7] The effect of additions, deletions, or key changes must be determined in context. Such techniques may influence the reader's opinion of the activity of the character or of the narrative itself. For example, when Sarah claims that Hagar is treating her unfairly, she states that Hagar looks upon her "with contempt" (16:5 RSV). This description of Hagar's behavior repeats the narrator's earlier statement about Hagar's feelings toward Sarah after Hagar became pregnant. By repeating the narrator's description, Sarah's judgment about Hagar's behavior is given credence.

The use of repetition may call special attention to God's involvement in a character's life or in the events of the narrative. God's promise to Hagar is reminiscent of the divine covenantal promise given to Abraham. This underscores the providential guidance given to Hagar, even though God's promise in this case does not constitute a covenant. Abraham's servant's repetition of the narrator's description of his actions reinforces the servant's own impetuousness. The narrator explains how the servant offered gifts to Rebekah before he was certain of her identity. However, when the servant later tells the story to Laban, he states that he inquired about Rebekah's origins before he offered the gifts. Moreover, in telling the instructions that Abraham gave him, the servant omits a crucial detail— that he could return without a bride if the woman was unwilling to accompany him back to Canaan. Instead, the servant tells Rebekah's family that he could return if the bride's family were unwilling to release her. This change introduces an element of suspense because Rebekah's family indeed does hesitate to let the daughter leave. Nonetheless, the servant's ultimate success points to the graciousness of God's protection. Similarly, when Rebekah presents her plan to Jacob to receive the blessing that Isaac designated for Esau, she repeats the words of Isaac's desire to bless his son. Significantly, she adds that the blessing will be done "before YHWH," thus emphasizing the fulfillment of God's plan.

Combination and Sequence of Narratives

The placement of narratives in a particular sequence often enables one text to comment upon the other. As Shimon Bar-Efrat states, "The narrative books of the Bible are not mere compilations of unconnected stories but, as is well known, are made up of sequences of narratives, which combine to constitute wider structures."[8] Sometimes such placement of texts emphasizes theological themes. For example, the account of Lot's egregious behavior toward his daughters and the birth of his rival descendants precedes the account of the birth of Abraham's heir. This dramatizes the estrangement between the peoples who were once companions. The genealogy of Rebekah comes immediately after God's testing of Abraham by instructing him to kill and then to spare his son Isaac. Isaac, who has escaped death, must now continue Abraham's lineage. The actual introduction to the person Rebekah follows the information that Sarah has died, again emphasizing that another woman will be necessary to continue the promise of descendants. Rebekah's preferential feelings toward her son Jacob are given after God's words to her proclaiming that he would be the designated heir to God's promises, suggesting that her feelings were influenced by God's revelation. The narrator discusses Esau's marriage to foreign women before Jacob and Rebekah deceive Isaac into giving Jacob the blessing, in order to show that Esau is not a worthy heir.

Narrative sequence is used also to emphasize the significance of a particular narrative. For example, the account of the rape of Dinah is both preceded and followed by descriptions of Jacob's relationship with potentially hostile people. In the preceding narrative, Jacob escapes trouble from Esau, and the two brothers are seemingly reconciled. In the account of the violent revenge upon the Shechemites that follows, however, the narrator shows that violence has escalated; God must intervene to protect Jacob from other threatening peoples. The narrative of Judah and Tamar comes after the account of Judah's crime against Joseph, wherein he convinced his brothers to sell Joseph for a profit, thereby preparing the reader for his additional unjust behavior toward his daughter-in-law. Potiphar's wife's attempt to seduce Joseph is placed after the account of Judah's wrongful withholding of his son for the levirate marriage in order to contrast two distinct kinds of sexual impropriety.

Type-scenes and Conventions

The use of certain scenes or descriptions prompts associations in the reader's mind because they are typically used in the Hebrew Bible to evoke specific expectations. For example, a young man who comes to a well will find a woman to be his bride. A patriarch who demands that his wife claim she is his sister will actually put her in threatening circumstances. A barren woman will eventually have a child due to God's intervention.

However, the narrator may also use type-scenes and conventions to raise certain expectations—only to shatter them. Thus, Lot's greeting of the angels at first parallels Abraham's gracious hospitality. Yet the narrator unfolds a very different scene in which Lot's attempts at hospitality go seriously awry. Abraham sends his servant to find a wife for Isaac; the hero himself does not go, and the risks of finding an acceptable bride as well as God's protective guidance are thus underscored. By using type-scenes and conventions, the narrator is able to weave various scenarios into a more comprehensive design and to support narrative and theological themes.[9]

Names and Epithets

The meaning of characters' names in biblical narratives often signifies crucial aspects of the person's role or his or her importance. Sometimes the narrator specifies the name's meaning. For example, Abram's name is changed by God to Abraham, meaning "father of many"—an obvious reference to God's promise that he would be the father of a great nation—however unlikely. Ishmael, which means "God hears," reflects God's promise to him and to his descendants and God's response to Hagar's plight. Leah and Rachel name their children according to the emotions they feel when their babies are born. The names of Leah's children reflect her frustration over Jacob's lack of love for her as well as her recognition that God has been gracious to her. For example, the names Simeon and Levi, associated respectively with the verbs "to hear" (*šmᶜ*) and "to be joined" (*lwh*), are understood to be related to Leah's poignant outcries. Of Simeon she states, "Because YHWH *has heard* that I am hated, he gave me this one also." Of Levi she cries, "Now this time my husband *will be joined* to me because I have borne him three sons." Rachel's naming of Joseph and Benoni mirrors both the pain of her past childlessness and the death that her last childbirth experience brings. Of Joseph, whose name is linked with the verb "to add" (*ysp*), she expresses the hope that God will add to her offspring and also states that God has taken away her reproach. Benoni, understood to mean "son of my affliction," is indicative of her impending death.

At other times, the meaning of the name is not specified, but would nonetheless be obvious to the Hebrew-speaking audience. Hence, "Leah" means "cow" and Rachel "ewe," two animals associated with fecundity. The name is appropriate to Leah, who is immediately fertile and prolific, yet ironic for Rachel, who experiences difficulty in conceiving. Furthermore, the meaning of a name can draw its significance from a play on words with another Hebrew word, irrespective of its legitimate linguistic association. Hence, "Hagar" echoes the word *gûr*, meaning "stranger" or "foreigner," appropriately associated with the woman who will never be integrated into Abraham's family. "Lot" is a play on words with "*him-mālēt*," meaning "delay," foreshadowing Lot's hesitancy to leave the city God has destined to destroy. Sometimes the significance of a name can be ironic. Onan, whose name means "vigorous," refuses to complete sexual intercourse with Tamar and is slain by God. Furthermore, the absence of a name may be significant. Potiphar's wife is never identified by name, which is appropriate because she is caricatured and stereotyped as a foreign temptress. Judah's wife, who is not named, plays no role in the story of Judah and his daughter-in-law Tamar. However, her identification as a "Canaanite" prompts the reader to question Judah's loyalty to his own family traditions and casts doubt on the character of his sons.

Epithets function like names; they express vital characteristics that will unfold in the development of the narrative. Thus, Sarah is identified as being "barren," a crucial problem for the promise of descendants. The epithet for Ishmael, a "wild ass," indicates the problematic relationship between the descendants of Sarah and Hagar. Rachel, "beautiful in form and beautiful to look at," quickly becomes the object of Jacob's passion. Not only are epithets used by the omniscient narrator, but also a character's use or nonuse of another's name can be relevant. When Sarai refers to Hagar she calls her "servant," thus stressing Hagar's subservient status. Jacob consistently is referred to as "Rebekah's son" whereas Esau is labelled "Isaac's son," signifying the parents' preferences. Laban calls Leah "this one" instead of by her name, reflecting the estrangement between father and daughter. As Meir Sternberg remarks, "the epithet is a ticking bomb, sure to explode into action in the narrator's (and God's) own good time." [10]

Diction

The narrator's word choice can be significant to develop dialogue, to foreshadow future events, to recall the past, or to present a particular perspective. It also has a powerful influence on the shaping of the reader's response to the character being discussed and for the interpretation of the narrative itself. Sometimes the narrator may have a character express his or her feelings with language that has powerful connotations. For example, when Sarah complains to Abraham that she has been mistreated by Hagar, she refers to Hagar's action as the "wrong" done to her. The word for "wrong" *(hamāśî)* always has violent connotations and is also used to describe Simeon and Levi's destruction of the Shechemites. When Rachel and Leah denounce Laban's behavior toward them, they claim that he has treated them as "foreigners" and has "devoured" their money. The term for "foreigners" connotes idolators, and "devour" connotes ruthless behavior. There is no doubt that these daughters despise their father's unjust treatment.

Sometimes the word choice of the narrator displays a clever double meaning. For example, Laban asks Jacob, "Should you serve me gratuitously?" (29:15) when he asks what payment would be appropriate. The word for "gratuitously" can also mean "in vain," which, of course, is exactly how Jacob serves Laban. The narrator identifies Potiphar as an officer of Pharaoh's guard. However, the word chosen for "officer" *(sārîs)* can also mean eunuch, suggesting that Potiphar's wife had a particular incentive to seek an extramarital sexual union.

On other occasions, the word chosen is particularly relevant for the narrative because of the associations it has in other texts in the Bible or because of its particular appropriateness for the narrative at hand. Thus, Abraham tells Sarah to make cakes with "choice flour" when the angels come to visit them, whereas Lot prepares the angels unleavened bread, recalling the bread made in haste in dire circumstances in Egypt. When God promises to return to Sarah to give her a child, she is told the event will recur in the spring *(kāʿēt ḥayyāh)*, literally, "the time when it is reviving" (18:10). This is a rare word used for spring, but appropriate since it underscores the crucial nature of the upcoming birth for the continuing of God's promise of descendants.

Setting

The locale of the narrative and movement of the characters within a specified territory not only develop the plot but also may heighten suspense, recall other events, or symbolize specific expectations, such as God's covenantal promises. When Abraham and Sarah go to Egypt to escape famine, the narrator foreshadows the threatening experience of the Israelites during the period of the Exodus by the location of the experience as well as by language that is used in the Exodus accounts. Lot's retreat to a cave symbolizes his inability to care for his daughters. Hagar's escape from Sarah, as well as her alienation from Abraham, bring her to the wilderness—a place where, in spite of its barrenness, God often intervenes.[11] Moreover, she first encounters the angel on the road to Shur, the region that will become the dwelling place of her son. Jacob's departure to the land of Nahor encourages the reader to see the precarious nature of the promise of land. Judah's movement into Canaanite territory may signify his turning away from his own family and customs.

In conclusion, narrative criticism proceeds by looking at a text as a consciously created artifact. Scenarios are not randomly sewn together but are crafted according to a particular perspective. The components of the narrator's art that we have surveyed are the means by which the narrator engages the audience to probe the details of any given narrative, to make connections with other texts, to challenge presuppositions or expectations, and to present a particular theological stance and commentary on human activities. These techniques are examined in greater detail in the following chapters on the women of Genesis.

2

Sarah

Carrier
of the Covenant

All students of the Bible know that God singles out Abraham (first known as Abram) for the promises of land, descendants, and blessing. God swears to Abraham that he will be the father of a great nation that will reside in Canaan.[1] It must also be noted, however, that the promise of descendants is not given only to Abraham. Not just any heir of Abraham will be the recipient of God's promise; rather, only the child born of Abraham and his first wife Sarah (first known as Sarai) will inherit God's covenantal promise. From the time that Abraham is introduced in the Genesis narrative until the first parcel of land is purchased by him, Sarah features prominently in the narrative. Although her story focuses upon her role as an ancestor of Israel and her difficulty in conceiving a child, her portrait is neither simplistic nor one-dimensional. Sarah is a woman who twice risks her well-being for her husband and future family and is also a fearful mother who casts out her servant, whom she perceives as a threat, because they cannot be reconciled.

Introduction to Sarai (Gen. 11:27-32)

Although Sarai's ancestry is not given, her introduction is striking none-theless.[2] The narrator juxtaposes the introduction and ancestry of Milcah (Abram's brother's wife) with the absence of ancestral information about Sarai.[3] Not only are her ancestors unknown, but the possibility of her

14

having descendants is doubtful. The narrator dramatically introduces Sarai's childlessness: "And it came to pass that Sarai was barren; she had no child" (11:30). The introductory phrase, "and it came to pass" *(wattĕhî)*, calls particular attention to Sarai's situation. Next, in two distinct phrases, the narrator twice informs the reader of Sarai's inability to conceive. It would be enough to use the epithet "Sarai was barren" *or* to state her circumstances, "she had no child"; the narrator emphasizes the seriousness of her plight by the repetition. Indeed, Sarai's childlessness is predominant in most of the scenes that concern her.

Sarai continues to be important after this stark introduction. Terah, the father of Abram, embarks on a journey to Canaan, but never completes it. He takes with him Abram and Sarai as well as his grandson Lot, who is identified for the second time in the text as the "son of Haran." By repeating the name of Lot's father and Lot's relationship to Terah, the narrator again draws attention to Sarai's barrenness. Terah has a grandson by his dead son Haran, but his living son Abram has provided no grandchildren through his wife Sarai. Yet, in spite of her childlessness, Sarai is part of the new people, called by God, who will receive the promise. The failure of the first attempted journey to Canaan by Terah is juxtaposed with the successful journey of Abram, Sarai, and Lot. Whereas Lot's participation in the promise will come to an end, Sarai will play a crucial role.[4]

God's Promises (Gen. 12:1-9)

God's promises to Abram of blessing, land, and descendants are first encountered in chapter 12, before the introduction of the term "covenant" *(berît)*, which ultimately becomes associated with the promises.[5] The narrator relates that God has spoken to Abram (12:1) and has appeared to him (12:7). These unequivocal terms leave no doubt that God has become inextricably bound to Abram and that he will receive great gifts.

In spite of this certainty of God's involvement with Abram, however, the narrative proceeds with dramatic suspense. From whom will Abram's descendants come? God does not address Sarai, nor does God tell Abram that Sarai will give him descendants. On the one hand, she is the most likely choice because the narrator specifically informs us that she accompanied Abram on his journey to Canaan. On the other hand, in the immediately preceding chapter, the narrator repeatedly referred to Sarai's barrenness. Intriguing references are introduced subtly: twice the narrator relates that Lot (Abram's nephew) accompanies Abram (12:4-5), and Abram is surrounded by "the persons that they had acquired in Haran" who have also come to Canaan (12:5). Might Abram's descendants come from someone other than Sarai? Lot and these unnamed persons from Haran stand as the first possibilities.

Abram and Sarai in Egypt (Gen. 12:10-20)

An oppressive famine produces a dramatic change of scene. God had promised Abram the land of Canaan, but Abram's fear that the famine will lead to his death compels him to go to Egypt. Once there, however, Abram again fears for his life, believing that the Egyptians will kill him in order to possess his beautiful wife. He thus devises a plan where Sarai must state that she is his sister to obtain favorable treatment for them from the Egyptians.

By the choice of locale and language, the narrator evokes the reader's recollection of the famine in Joseph's day and Joseph's subsequent residence in Egypt, which eventually lead to the Israelites' slavery. The introductory phrase, "Now there was a famine in the land" (12:10), foreshadows the famine that had prompted Joseph's brothers to seek refuge in Egypt: "There was famine in all the lands" (41:54). Furthermore, the famine of Abram's day was "oppressive" (*kāvēd*), a word used three times to describe the famine in Joseph's time (43:1; 47:4, 13). More obvious are the references to Pharaoh and the plagues that recall the Exodus. The narrator's audience would be familiar with these references to tragedies in the history of Israel, and therefore concern for the fate of Abram and Sarai is heightened.

As the narrative progresses, the reader's sympathies are drawn increasingly toward Sarai and less toward Abram. Although it is understandable that Abram is concerned for his life in a strange area, he surprisingly shows no concern for Sarai's welfare. Rather, he imagines the worst for himself, fearing that the Egyptians will take every opportunity to treat him cruelly. He expects that they will treat Sarai as an object and therefore will say, "This is his wife" (12:12), and that they will kill him. By using "this" (*zō’t*) instead of "she" or "Sarai," the narrator emphasizes Sarai's objectification. Similarly, the word employed by the narrator for "kill" (*hārag*), which is best translated "slay," connotes ruthless brutality and is used to draw attention to Abram's exaggerated fears. For example, *hārag* is used in Genesis to describe Cain's slaying of Abel (4:8), Esau's plan to murder his brother (27:41), and the mass slaying of the men of Shechem by Simeon and Levi (34:25-26). Abram devises the plan so that all will be to his advantage; thus, he states to Sarai: "Please say you are my sister, so that it may go well with *me* for your sake and that *my soul* may live on your account."[6]

While it is true that Sarai is an accomplice in Abram's plan, the narrator shows that her role is due more to her powerlessness than to her willing agreement.[7] Abram's language demonstrates his concern for himself, with no regard for Sarai. Sarai does not speak in this account, and the narrator comments neither on her feelings, her response, nor on what she says to Pharaoh. Her silence is not an indication of complicity, but rather a testimony to her powerlessness. Sarai is not so much an accomplice as a silent object.[8]

As expected, Pharaoh is told that Sarai is Abram's sister. It is important to note, however, that when Pharaoh discovers the deception, he cites what *Abram* has said to him (12:19). From this important detail the narrator reveals that it is Abram alone who undoubtedly deceives Pharaoh. Whether Sarai also did so is not specified, further emphasizing her lack of power.

Abram's questionable judgment is contrasted with Pharaoh's behavior. From the beginning of this scene, the narrator presents Pharaoh as a just man. Under the impression that Sarai is Abram's sister, he not only lets the foreigners live, but he also bestows upon Abram generous gifts. Even more importantly, it is Pharaoh, and not Abram, who is concerned about the consequences of adultery. Pharaoh discerns that the plagues were sent because of Sarai's exploitation. The narrator does not state that Pharaoh explicitly regarded the plagues as a punishment for his actions, but this is implied by the placement of his exasperated remarks immediately after the description that the plagues have begun.[9] Nevertheless, when Pharaoh remonstrates against Abram, he does not mention the hardship of the plagues but rather stresses the wrong of Abram's action.[10]

The narrator highlights Pharaoh's anger by his impassioned speech. He speaks quickly, in a series of accusatory statements that leave Abram no time to respond. Indeed, Abram can only remain silent as he faces an accuser who is completely correct in charging him, "What is this you have done to me? Why did you not tell me that she is your wife? Why did you say, 'She is my sister,' so that I took her to me as a wife? So now, here is your wife, take and go!" (12:18-19). In these two verses Pharaoh never mentions Sarai by name, but instead stresses her relationship to Abram; she is his wife *(ʔištēhā)*. The narrator indicates that Pharaoh is so shocked that Abram would exploit his wife that he can only express his disbelief in the repetition of these similar phrases. Finally, the narrator words Pharaoh's demand that Abram leave in such a way that reveals his repulsion.

Pharaoh demands that Abram leave immediately, stating literally, "Take and go!" The verb for "take" (*lāqaḥ*) normally requires an object or prepositional phrase. By omitting it, the narrator conveys impassioned speech.[11]

Sarai has been victimized throughout this account, first by her husband who hastily decides to use her to thwart potential danger to himself, then by Pharaoh who unwittingly takes her as a wife. It is true that the narrator does not specifically say that Pharaoh had sexual intercourse with Sarai; but the ambiguity does remain as a permanent gap. The normal term to express sexual intercourse would be "he went in to her." Instead, the narrator reports in Pharaoh's direct speech, "I took her to me as a wife" (12:19). This phrase clearly has sexual connotations; it is the same phrase used, for example, when Sarai gives Hagar to Abram as a wife.[12] By leaving the situation unresolved, however, the narrator is able to emphasize the danger to Sarai without causing undue scandal.

The account of the first ancestors in Egypt seems at first to end benignly, but in fact the narrator hints at the lasting consequences that this sojourn will have for Abram and Sarai. Abram left not only with Sarai, but with "all that he had" (12:20). This phrase undoubtedly includes the gifts from Pharaoh such as the "menservants and maidservants" (12:16). The term chosen for maidservants, *šepāḥōt*, is found next when it is used of Hagar.[13] It is possible that the narrator wants the reader to consider that Sarai's trouble with Hagar, whose ancestry was Egyptian, has its roots in this sojourn in Egypt. Other interpreters see Abram's escape with such wealth as an indication of the ethically ambiguous nature of this narrative.[14] It is more likely, however, that what he takes with him foreshadows the difficulties that lie ahead with Sarai and Hagar.

Sarai's Plan to Have a Child (Gen. 16:1-6)

This next section concerning Sarai follows immediately upon the narration of the covenantal promise for descendants and land made to Abram in chapter 15. The opening statement of chapter 16 is striking. The narrator juxtaposes the divine promises with Sarai's barrenness and introduces an intriguing detail: "Now Sarai, the wife of Abram, did not bear him a child, but she had an Egyptian maid, and her name was Hagar" (16:1). The word used to identify Hagar as Sarai's servant, *šiphāh*, is the same term used in chapter 12 to describe the servants Abram obtained from Pharaoh.[15] The narrator has posed an important question by placing these two phrases together. What role will Hagar play in Sarai's struggle to have a child?

Indeed, the sentence that immediately follows reveals Sarai's plan.[16] Eschewing the use of Hagar's name, Sarai tells Abram to have intercourse with her "servant" and states, "Perhaps I will be built up through her" (16:2). The phrase "build up" does in fact refer to having a child, but it more importantly refers to establishing a people. It is said, for example, that Rachel and Leah have "built up" Israel (Ruth 4:11) and that God will "build up" David (2 Sam. 7:27)—meaning that a dynasty has been established. Sarai hopes that perhaps her descendants will come from Hagar, who will act as a surrogate mother. Yet the narrator will reveal clearly that the mere occasion of the birth of a child is insignificant for Sarai's having descendants. Indeed, the fact that Hagar has a child will actually threaten Sarai's descendants.

The narrator relates the information about Sarai's plan thus far without commenting on its significance. Was she justified in having Abram go to Hagar? No answer is given, although the narrator does pause to add the detail that at this point Sarai and Abram lived in Canaan ten years without having children. In addition, there has been an undetermined amount of time before they came to Canaan. Surely after ten years of Sarai trying to have a child the reader's sympathies are with her as she takes steps to do something about it.

In contrast to the great amount of time that passes without Sarai's having a child, Hagar conceives the first time that Abram has sexual relations with her. The narrator suggests that immediately after the pregnancy began, a dispute arose between Hagar and Sarai. After she becomes pregnant, Hagar disdains Sarai. The narrator explains, "When she saw that she conceived, her mistress became contemptible in her eyes" (16:4). The word for "became contemptible" or "became lightly esteemed" (*kālal*) expresses disdain for human beings when they do something significantly wrong. In 1 Sam. 2:30, for example, an unnamed prophet declares that those who despise God will be "lightly esteemed." Similarly, Nah. 1:14 states that Assyrian idols will be cut off and a grave will be made for the people because they are "contemptible." When Job recognizes that he has been wrong in challenging God, he declares that he is "of small account" or "contemptible" (Job 40:4). This is the predominant meaning of the word throughout the Hebrew Bible. The narrator thus indicates that Hagar used her pregnancy to antagonize Sarai.[17]

There are two other instances of surrogate motherhood in the Hebrew Bible that can be contrasted with the presentation of the experience of Sarah and Hagar. Both Bilhah and Zilpah give birth to children who are considered the descendants of Rachel and Leah. There is nothing in those stories to indicate that their function was aberrant or controversial. There is no indication that Bilhah or Zilpah protested or confronted Rachel or Leah.[18] Indeed, the stories are related without conflict, and the maidservants stay with their mistresses indefinitely. In presenting the stories of Hagar and Sarai, the narrator shows sympathy for and criticism of both, but the judgments given do not come from the situation of surrogacy per se. It must be remembered that although Abram has heard that he will have descendants, God does not specify that Sarai will have his child until after Hagar has a child (Genesis 17). Neither Sarai nor Abram is privy to God's plan for the couple to have a child at the time when Sarai suggests that she have a child through Hagar.

The narrator demonstrates that Sarai's plan continues to cause strife and discontent but uses language that shows that both women suffer. Sarai learns quickly that the surrogacy plan is doomed, and the contention between Hagar and Sarai escalates. Sarai holds Abram responsible for Hagar's treatment of her, and a rift develops between Sarai and Abram as is evident by the strong language with which she addresses him. Sarai's first words to her husband are accusatory. She exclaims: "May the wrong done to me be upon you" (16:5). The word choice for "wrong" *(hămāśî)* always has violent connotations. In Genesis it is used to describe the earth before God's destruction of it by the flood (6:11, 13) and to indicate the violence done by Simeon and Levi when they ruthlessly destroy the Shechemites. By the choice of this word, the narrator emphasizes the egregious wrong done to Sarai.[19] When Sarai describes to Abram what Hagar has done to her, she repeats the phrase that the narrator used to describe Hagar's feelings toward her—that she has become "a trifling." By this repetition, the narrator legitimizes Sarai's estimation of the problem.[20] Sensing that this controversy is insoluble, Sarai proclaims, "May YHWH judge between you and me" (16:5). This phrase is used of God to decide controversy, and it is important to note that the one who invokes it is normally judged by the narrator to be innocent.[21] The narrator is aware that Hagar will endure a difficult plight because of Sarai, but the narrator refrains from portraying the conflict simplistically. Although Sarai clearly has power over Hagar, each woman contributes to the other's suffering, as does Abram who is steadfast in refusing to be involved. He returns Hagar to Sarai. Now Sarai's own pain has become destructive. She afflicts Hagar, who flees from her.

The narrator does not make unnuanced judgments about the behavior of the women in this narrative. The choice of words and the actions of the characters themselves indicate that their motives are complex. Hagar's response when Sarai first gives her to Abram is never revealed. Did she protest? Or did she think of this as an elevation of her status? What is clear is that once she became pregnant, she "held Sarai in contempt." Was Sarai's outrage justified? The narrator is sensitive to Sarai's frustration, yet the poignancy of Hagar's plight is recognized as well. The story of Hagar is examined in chapter 4. It is important to note that Sarai knows at this point she will not be "built up" through Hagar. By preserving the complexities of this situation, the narrator poignantly presents the difficulties in addressing the painful situations of two women: one who deeply suffers the pain of childlessness, the other who suffers because of the childless woman's desperation.

The Changing of Sarai's Name (Gen. 17:15-22)

Upon completion of the scene where Sarai remains childless, yet where Hagar is promised a son, Abram receives God's covenantal promise once more that he has been made "the father of a multitude of peoples" (17:5). In this context, Abram's name is changed to Abraham, meaning "father of many." Indeed, God promises him, "I will establish my covenant between me and you and your descendants after you throughout their generations for an everlasting covenant, to be God to you and to your descendants after you" (17:7 RSV). At this point in the narrative, the reader is led to assume that the only woman through whom Abraham will have descendants is Hagar. However, a dramatic reversal to Sarai's situation is planned by God. Indeed, the narrator relates the message unequivocally by employing God's perspective: God announces the plan to Abraham. God first changes her name as a preview to her function. Her name change to "Sarah" is understood in popular etymology to mean "princess" and thus points to her similar role as a mother of an important people.[22]

It is most striking that although God reveals to Abraham that Sarah will have a child, Abraham refuses to believe it. Twice the phrase "I will bless her" introduces the pronouncement. First God says, "I will bless her, and furthermore I will give you a son by her," and secondly God proclaims, "And I will bless her, and she will bring forth nations; rulers of peoples will come from her" (17:16). These phrases echo the promises given to Abraham. He, too, is told he would be "the father of a multitude of peoples" and that "rulers will come forth from you" (17:5-6).

The narrator casts doubt on Abraham's willingness to accept God's messages by describing his response from his own perspective. Abraham has a direct revelation wherein he hears of Sarah's name change and is told twice of her role as ancestress. Nonetheless, Abraham falls to the ground in order to laugh to himself and expressly questions his ability and that of the aged Sarah to have a child. Although he does not repeat his doubts aloud to God, he dares to propose an alternative, asking God to allow Ishmael to be the inheritor of the covenant. God refuses and adds specific information to the revelation that a son will be born to Sarah. The son will be named Isaac; he will have descendants that will be given the covenant; and he will be born in the same season of the following year.

When this revelation is completed, Abraham circumcizes the men of his household, as he is commanded, but at this point the narrator introduces an important gap. Abraham does not inform Sarah of God's promise that they will have a child. Indeed, the narrator closes the gap in the next scene when it will become clear that Sarah first learns of the promise only when she overhears another conversation between God's messengers and Abraham. Esther Fuchs argues that because the revelation of the change of Sarai's name was given to Abraham instead of to Sarah herself, Sarah is shown to be in a subordinate position.[23] However, the narrator uses the revelation to Abraham to develop a crucial aspect of the story. The narrator underscores Abraham's questioning and doubting by revealing his questioning of God about the wisdom of God's plan. By withholding this information from Sarah, Abraham's continuing doubt is underscored, whereas Sarah cannot be expected to anticipate God's words about her upcoming role.[24] Thus, the reader is prepared to understand Sarah's disbelief in the following scene.

God's Encounter with Abraham and Sarah
(Gen. 18:1-15)

When God appears as three visitors to Abraham and Sarah, Abraham first responds as a solicitous host.[25] The importance of the visit is emphasized when Abraham speaks to Sarah in impassioned, abbreviated speech: "Hurry! Three measures of choice flour! Knead and make cakes!" (18:6). By employing language that foreshadows the hasty flight of the Israelites from Egypt, the narrator suggests that another dramatic development in the history of the Israelite people is at hand.

Some commentators have interpreted the announcement of Sarah's pregnancy as a doublet of the previous account, when Sarah's name change and her future as the covenantal carrier are announced. Whatever the independent origins of these two scenes, the narrator links them as one continuous narrative, and in so doing reveals another step in the process by which Sarah becomes Isaac's mother.[26] For the first time, God visits Abraham and Sarah while they are together. At first, the messengers ask Abraham about the whereabouts of Sarah, whom they expressly identify as Abraham's wife (18:9). God addresses the next statement to Abraham alone, saying, "I will indeed return to you in the spring" (18:10). The unexpected and unique role of God in this pregnancy is emphasized by the narrator's word choice to describe the season. The phrase used is *kāᶜēt ḥayyāh*—the "time when it is reviving,"—i.e., the spring. This term rarely is used, found only in 2 Kings 4:16, 17 where the prophet Elisha promises the Shunamite woman, who like Sarah also has an elderly husband, that she will have a son in "the time when it is reviving." This unique phrase highlights the unexpected quality of the pregnancy of this long-infertile woman.

The narrator subtly prepares us for Sarah's response to the words of God by the description of Sarah's location, by the repetition of her situation, and by a sympathetic view of her own perspective. The narrator states that "Sarah was listening at the door of the tent; it was behind him" (18:10). In an important parenthetical statement, the narrator reveals that the couple not only was old, but that "it had ceased to be with Sarah as the way of women" (18:11)—a reference indicating that her menstrual periods had stopped; presumably she was incapable of pregnancy. Like Abraham before her, Sarah laughs and expresses her doubts to herself. In a moving phrase Sarah states, "After I am worn out *(bĕlōtî)*, shall I have pleasure?—and my lord is old" (18:12). The choice of the term "worn out" highlights not only her physical years, but the painful results of her childlessness. By using the phrase, "have pleasure," instead of the more direct "have a child," the narrator is able to imply the several consequences of her experience. Because the word can have sexual connotations, one possibility of its meaning is that Abraham never responds sexually to Sarah. Another would be that her infertility has made her life so bleak that pleasure is not possible. Finally, it can refer to emotional pain or the social stigma of not having children. The narrator first reveals Sarah's perspective in her direct words, and then shows Sarah's perspective on Abraham. Sarah's reference to Abraham's age suggests that even he is too old to have a child. By using the term "lord/master" to refer to Abraham, the narrator shows Sarah's dependence on her husband; having a child is not contingent only on Sarah's capabilities anymore. The final perspective on the importance of Sarah's laughter is given from God's own view. In quoting what Sarah said about her own laughter to Abraham, God says, "Why did Sarah laugh, and say, 'Shall I indeed have a child, now that I am old?' Is anything too awesome for YHWH?" (18:13-14). By using "have a child" instead of "have pleasure," the narrator shows that, from God's perspective, the most crucial aspect of Sarah's difficulties lies precisely in her inability to have a child, a situation that God is now about to rectify.

It is obvious from this account that this is the first time Sarah has learned about God's promise to her. God continues to address Abraham concerning Sarah and demands that he account for Sarah's laughter. Sarah dramatically interrupts, making her presence known and feebly attempting to protect Abraham. Sarah, who has not been addressed by God, claims that she did not laugh.²⁷ The narrator does not judge Sarah harshly for this deception, but relates, from the omniscient viewpoint, that she acted "because she was afraid" (18:15). Indeed, unlike Abraham who so doubted that he asked God for an alternative plan for legitimate descendants, Sarah does not press the point when remonstrated by God. Perhaps because she recognizes that it is wrong she simply denies it. Curiously, some of the sexist interpretations of the past exonerate Abraham for laughing (in chapter 17), but condemn Sarah.²⁸

Interlude on the Destruction of Sodom and Gomorrah (Gen. 18:16—19:38)

When the messengers leave Abraham and Sarah, they continue on their journey and encounter Lot in Sodom. These sections of the Biblical narrative are investigated in the following chapter. It is important to note at this point in the investigation of Sarah, however, that after Lot is saved from Sodom, he becomes the father of two nations of people who later struggle with Israel during much of the nations' histories.²⁹ Thus, by the placement of this account of Lot and his daughters within the Abraham and Sarah narrative, the narrator draws attention to the enemies of Israel who gain a stronghold even before Abraham's legitimate heir is born.

Abimelech's Potential Threat to Sarah (Gen. 20:1-18)

The narrator once again employs the type-scene of the ancestress who encounters danger. As in Sarah's earlier encounter with Pharaoh (12:10-20), Abraham tells Sarah once more to pose as his sister so they might find favor in strange territory.³⁰ The significance of this narrative is enhanced by the context. Sarah, the future mother of Israel, will have a child within a year's time.³¹ Any adulterous relationship at this time would have more serious consequences because her pregnancy is now imminent.[32] The narrator includes details that show Abraham's actions to be highly questionable, and the reader wonders why he puts Sarah in danger again.

Unlike the earlier account, when famine compels the couple to travel, the narrator gives no reason for the sojourn in Gerar.[33] Moreover, Abraham does not explain his plan.[34] He does not express to Sarah the fear that he might be exploited because of her beauty as he did when he approached Egypt. By omitting these details, the narrator casts doubt upon Abraham's later explanations to Abimelech.

Throughout the account, the narrator stresses God's intervention in Abraham's potentially disastrous plan. In Sarah's earlier interlude with Pharaoh, the reader is led to believe that she stays with him for a while, certainly more than one day, before Pharaoh recognizes that the plagues have something to do with the sojourners. However, in the present story, Abimelech learns the very same evening that he has done wrong. God appears to Abimelech in a dream on the very same night in which he meets Sarah. Whereas Pharaoh learned indirectly, Abimelech learns directly from God that Sarah is "a husband's wife" (*bĕʿulat bāʿal*, 20:3). God initially condemns Abimelech to death, but the narrator unequivocally explains, from the omniscient perspective, that Abimelech did not touch Sarah. Abimelech's words are well chosen. He appeals to God's sense of justice and professes his innocence. He shows that both Abraham and Sarah lied to him and he employs a solemn oath to reiterate his innocence.[35]

The narrator argues a carefully constructed case that Abimelech is indeed innocent of touching Sarah. The statement is not only made by the narrator's omniscient voice, but also from God's perspective. God proclaims "It was I who prevented you from sinning against me; therefore I did not allow you to touch her" (20:6). By presenting proof in God's words as well as in the third person, the narrator presents incontrovertible evidence that Abimelech never had sexual relations with Sarah. After Abimelech responds to God honestly and passionately, God agrees that Abimelech will not be condemned to death if Sarah is restored to Abraham.

By providing the details of Abimelech's activity after he receives God's revelation, the narrator underscores his good intentions and sincerity. The narrator states that when Abimelech "got up the next morning" (20:8), he immediately called all his servants. Just as Abimelech responded to God with utmost seriousness, so too do the servants fear God. The narrator shows, with increasing evidence, that Abraham had no cause to fear for his life at the hands of Abimelech's people.

After informing the servants, Abimelech immediately calls Abraham. In a series of pointed questions, he berates Abraham four times, without even pausing to hear his reply. Only in the last question does he leave time for Abraham to answer, demanding, "What were you thinking, that you did this thing?" (20:10).

Abraham, speaking for the first time since he said, "She is my sister" (20:2), responds with weak excuses. Abraham claims he perpetrated the deception because there was "no fear of God in this place" (20:11). However, the narrator indicates that there was in fact substantial fear of God on the part of both Abimelech and his servants. Abraham's words are suspect. He claims that Sarah is actually his half-sister, but this is confirmed neither by the narrator nor by any other dialogue or genealogical source either before or after this scene. By introducing this permanent gap, the narrator implies that Abraham's veracity can be doubted. Indeed, throughout this narrative, Abraham gives inaccurate information, especially when he states that God "caused me to wander" (20:13).[36] The word used here, *hit'û*, not only means "cause to wander," but also may mean "cause to err" or "mislead."[37] This terminology of Abraham's contradicts the narrative that states that God led Abraham to Canaan. Thus the reader's doubts are raised as to Abraham's credibility. Did he really tell Sarah to claim she was his sister "in every place" (20:13) as he maintains he did to Abimelech here? Abraham's excuses arouse skepticism, whereas Abimelech appears trusting, honest, and legitimately angry with Abraham's lies.[38]

Abimelech's good intentions are demonstrated by the manner in which he responds to Abraham after Abraham's attempts to justify his actions. Abimelech restores Sarah to Abraham, as God commanded him, but he also gives generous gifts. He even appears naive, referring to Abraham as Sarah's brother while addressing her.[39] Although the translation and meaning of the Hebrew are difficult, the context suggests that Abimelech gives gifts either in order to vindicate Sarah's innocence or to avoid God's anger.[40]

Past studies have compared the account of Sarah and Abraham's encounter with Pharaoh (chapter 12) to this encounter with Abimelech (chapter 20) and have maintained that the latter reveals a unique "moralizing" strand. Authors of such studies correctly have pointed out that the story in Genesis 12 is ambiguous as to whether Pharaoh had sexual relations with Sarah, while the account in Genesis 20 goes to great lengths to show that Abimelech did not touch her. They conclude that Genesis 20 must be a deliberate rewriting of chapter 12, undertaken to address the ambiguities of Sarah's encounter with Pharaoh. Such arguments, however, are not convincing. The story of Genesis 20 does not erase the ambiguity of Sarah's earlier encounter with Pharaoh. Indeed, the two narratives function distinctly. In Genesis 12, there is little or no chance that Sarah would become pregnant even if Pharaoh did have relations with her. When chapter 20 is reached, the reader knows that Sarah will have a child in less than a year. God has promised Abraham twice, and Sarah finally learns of the promise when she overhears the divine conversation with Abraham. Indeed, the account that immediately follows tells of Sarah's pregnancy and the birth of Isaac. Thus, Abraham is fully culpable in allowing Sarah to be with another man. If she had stayed with Abimelech, the father of her child would have been in doubt. In order to remove any question, the narrator must stress that Sarah was never approached sexually by Abimelech. The narrator succeeds in showing that Abimelech understands the immorality of adultery more readily than Abraham. Moreover, God is shown to be more protective of Sarah than when she had been in Pharaoh's court; the reason, it appears, is the promise that she will soon have a child.

The Long-awaited Birth of Isaac (Gen. 21:1-14)

In this chapter the narrator shows that God is a keeper of promises. The narrator uses four phrases in the first sentence to stress God's intervention in Sarah's ability to conceive. God "visited Sarah" as God "had said." God "did to Sarah" as God "had spoken" (21:1). The narrator emphasizes the role of God as keeper of the earlier promises to Abraham and Sarah by including the time reference; Sarah bore her son "at the appointed time which God had spoken" (21:2). Abraham and Sarah's past reactions to God's promises are also underscored. Abraham's naming of Isaac recalls the earlier associations of the couple's laughter over God's promise of a son. Although Abraham conducts the naming and the circumcision, Sarah features prominently in this first scene as well. In the first seven sentences, her name is used six times. Her response is one of joy and personal triumph. The naming of her child Isaac not only reflects the occasions when his parents laughed in disbelief, but also represents the laughter of ecstasy and relief. Her words imply that no one will again be able to deride her for being childless, but they also indicate that she recognizes the incredible reality that she has conceived and given birth.

After the birth, circumcision, and naming are described, the scene shifts to another joyous occasion: Isaac is weaned, and Abraham prepares a feast. Unexpectedly, our preconceptions for this happy event are shattered. In a stunning move, the narrator has the reader learn of the impending difficulties through Sarah's observations. Sarah first becomes somber when she sees "the son of Hagar the Egyptian, whom she had born to Abraham, playing" (21:9).[41] The narrator has already indicated Ishmael's lower status by eliminating his name in the description of the scene. Nonetheless, Sarah recognizes that he remains Abraham's son and her fears surface. She confronts Abraham, demanding: "Cast out this slave woman and her son; for the son of this slave woman shall not be heir with my son, with Isaac" (21:10). The narrator eliminates the names of both Ishmael and Hagar when Sarah speaks of them, thereby emphasizing the strength of Sarah and Isaac over the powerlessness of Hagar and Ishmael.

Most commentators assume that the narrator's statement of Abraham's feelings indicates that he sympathizes with Ishmael. However, the narrator is operating much more subtly, preserving the complexities of the struggle between Sarah and Hagar. The narrator states: "And the matter (*haddābar*) was very displeasing to Abraham on account of his son" (21:11). The matter could refer either to Sarah's desire to dismiss Hagar or to the existence of the threat to Isaac. If the former is true, the son would refer to Ishmael; but if the latter is true, the son would refer to Isaac.[42] If there is any doubt as to whether Sarah's plan is justified, the narrator has God respond in a direct revelation to Abraham. Once again Abraham is reminded that his descendants will be given through Isaac. God confirms Sarah's plan; perhaps she understands God's will better than did Abraham all along.[43] Complying with God's demands, Abraham prepares Hagar to depart. (Hagar's plight is examined in chapter 4.)

The narrator does not mention Sarah's activities again. Her most important role has been as the mother of the people who inherit the promises first given to Abraham. In presenting her struggle to have a child, the narrator shows great sensitivity. It is clear that the narrator is aware that the very existence of Israel is precarious. Its beginnings as a people are fragile and Israel is threatened by another people. It is true, of course, that the Israelites were in contention with various peoples, including the children of Ishmael, when they struggled for their own independent existence.[44] It is difficult to assess exactly what the narrator's audience would have thought about the Ishmaelites, but most indications are that they were considered enemies. References in other parts of the Hebrew Bible show the Ishmaelites to be equated with the Midianites, who sold Joseph into slavery in Egypt, who employed Balaam to curse Israel, whose idolatry influenced Israel, and against whom Gideon had to defend Israel.[45] Yet, the narrator does not portray this enemy of the people of Israel as an entity completely alien from themselves. The Ishmaelites are closely related to the Israelites. They share the same father! It is tempting for nations to present a caricature of their enemies, but here the narrator presents a sophisticated understanding: the people who are hostile to Israel are also very much like the Israelites. Although Sarah and Isaac enjoy Abraham's protection and God's covenantal promises, Israel also recognizes that its triumphs may cause the suffering of others.

The Death and Burial of Sarah (Gen. 23:1-17)

Even in her death, Sarah continues to play a role in securing her people's inheritance. In procuring a burial site for Sarah, Abraham negotiates a purchase of land from the Hittites, which becomes the foundation of the Israelites' title to the land in the Hebron area.

Of all the ancestresses, only Sarah's age is given at her death. Her life of 127 years is noteworthy and can be compared to the long life spans of the patriarchs. Abraham dies at age 175, Isaac at 180, and Jacob at 147.[46]

Abraham's mourning for Sarah is underscored by the narrator in two distinct phrases. The narrator reports that he "went in to mourn for Sarah," and also "to cry for her" (23:2). This simple description points to Abraham's genuine loss.

Although Sarah will no longer figure in Abraham's life, her death prompts him to procure an important title to the land. The narrator describes in great detail Abraham's insistence that he pay for the land, and that it not be simply received as a gift. Only after three lengthy negotiations do the Hittites agree to sell the land. The narrator also describes the transaction of the sale so that there is no question that Abraham legally obtained it.

In the final summation of this account the narrator recalls Sarah's role: "Abraham buried his wife Sarah in the cave of the field of Machpelah across from Mamre, which is Hebron, in the land of Canaan" (23:19). Although all of the land of Canaan was promised to Abraham by God, this is the first instance in Genesis where Abraham has legal possession of a portion of it. Sarah's death plays a genuine part in Abraham's procurement of this portion of the covenantal promise.

Conclusions

Although the covenantal promises are never specifically given to Sarah, it is important to note that the narratives about her show that she plays a crucial role in the birth of the people of Israel. Her portrait has both personal and national import. She is shown to be a woman who must endure great suffering, but who also was driven to maltreat Hagar. The consequences of being childless in a culture that held male children in such esteem cannot be fully appreciated in our modern society. Nonetheless, the pain of being childless still crosses boundaries and can be felt by all women who experience the sadness of infertility. On one level, Sarah's suffering comes to an end: Isaac is born. However, Sarah's strength and drive that lead her to give Hagar to Abraham also lead to tragedy because the legacy of Hagar and Ishmael causes future suffering.

3

The Daughters of Lot

Victims of Their Father's Abuse

Like many women in the Bible, the daughters of Lot are presented as peripheral characters, and only remnants of their story survive. Because their story focuses on two important events, the accounts of these nameless daughters, who must take their identities from their father, are preserved. The first event is shocking; the daughters are threatened with sexual abuse by the entire male population of a city. The second event is equally dramatic; the childless daughters become pregnant by their own father.

Sexuality and sexual violence are frequently discussed and regulated in the Hebrew Scriptures in narrative and legal texts. In these accounts of Lot's daughters, the narrator's explicit views about the potential violence to them and their incestuous relationship are not directly revealed; nonetheless, the development of the narrative itself presents a powerful portrait of the effects of threatened sexual violence. Most modern commentators recognize that the proposed sodomy against the (male) angels is portrayed as reprehensible, yet they have been sympathetic to Lot's actions toward his daughters.[1] Rather than condemn the offer of his daughters as rape victims, they point to the mitigating circumstances, the demands of hospitality, which putatively excuse his behavior.

In describing the events that lead to Lot's actions, however, the narrator shows that Lot is, in fact, unjust in the treatment of his daughters. He not only threatens them by suggesting to the townsmen that they be abused, but he also abdicates his responsibility to provide for their welfare after the destruction of Sodom. His abnegation of responsibility is critical. Driven by their isolation and sense of hopelessness, the daughters plan to have children through their father. The descendants of Lot and his daughters are continually in strife with the descendants of Abraham and Sarah. The trajectory of the story of Lot's life demonstrates that Lot falls from his more noble beginnings. He evolves from a man who journeys to Canaan with Abraham and Sarah to a man who leads a corrupt existence in Sodom where he no longer can be categorized as one of the righteous. By examining the entirety of the texts about him, the reader can assess the few remarks about his daughters and determine his relationship with them.[2]

Introduction to Lot (Gen. 11:31)

The reader first encounters Lot as a member of Abram's extended family (11:31). Lot's father Haran is identified as Abram's brother and thus Lot's relationship as Abram's nephew is established. Little else is known about him or his wife and family. Since Lot appears within the context of the introduction to the Abram cycle, one may surmise that he will play an important role. His importance, however, is not what might be expected. He is not included in any of the covenantal promises to Abraham, nor is he present at any of the revelatory scenes of God and Abraham. The man who is identified by the narrator as the first companion of Abraham on his trip to Canaan soon becomes his antagonist.

Lot's Conflict with Abram (Gen. 13:5-13)

The conflict between Abram and Lot leads to strife and to the separation of the two newcomers to the land over which their herdsmen quarrel. Some commentators suggest that the chief significance of the separation of Lot and Abram in chapter 13 is that Lot is excluded as Abram's heir to the covenantal promise.[3] However, the crisis does not center on who is Abram's heir. Rather, it concerns the promise of land to Abram and the consequences for Lot, who argues that he, too, must have a part of it.[4] The dispute is resolved by partition; at the end of the chapter the reader finds that Abram and Lot each reside in separate territories.

The promise of land is first threatened by the contentious nature of the herdsmen. Abram takes the role of peacemaker. Although the narrative refers only to "a dispute between the herdsmen of Abram's cattle and the herdsmen of Lot's cattle" (13:7), Abram is most concerned about the actual or potential discord between himself and Lot. Abram's words to Lot demonstrate his desire for peace: "Let there be no dispute between you and me," he states (13:8). Abram then suggests that he and Lot be separated *(hippāred nā² mēʿālāy,* 13:9). Abram's suggestion is recorded in direct speech; he generously and unselfishly offers Lot the first selection of the best land.[5]

The text does not record Lot's response to Abram. However, the description of his view of the land is indicative of his selfishness in selecting his portion. Observing that "the entire plain of the Jordan—all of it—was well-watered like the garden of YHWH, like the land of Egypt" (13:10), he chooses "the entire plain of the Jordan" for himself (13:11). The narrator indicates that Lot is concerned more with procuring the best land than in coming to an amicable settlement with Abram.

The narrator hints at problems that are later associated with Lot and his daughters in Sodom by the description of Lot's view of the land and his initial journey to settle in the region. The narrator identifies not only Sodom and Gomorrah in the description of Lot's sighting of the land, but also introduces Zoar, a city whose significance to Lot will soon become apparent. Although Lot chose the Transjordan because it was fertile, the reader knows that the land in fact is not well-watered anymore and that its barrenness comes from God's decision to destroy the region after Lot settled there. The narrator contrasts Abram's dwelling in Canaan with Lot's perspective on the land and his settlement in Sodom where the men "were evil, and were sinners against YHWH" (13:13). Thus, the distance between Abram and Lot is not only a geographic one.

Lot's Predicament (Gen. 14:1-16)

As the next scene continues, it becomes apparent that the conflict between Abram and Lot over their possessions is not the most serious threat to Abraham. The land of Sodom and Gomorrah, which Lot has chosen for himself, is replete with conflict and war.[6] Abraham undertakes a risky military venture to save Lot, and the reader is relieved to learn that he succeeds in obtaining Lot's release and in securing his own safe return.

Lot's Conspicuous Absence
(Gen. 14:17—19:1)

After this incident, Lot is conspicuously absent from the next four chapters of the Abram cycle. By interrupting the Lot cycle with these scenes from the Abram narratives, the narrator shows that the man who accompanied Abram from Ur and chose to live in Sodom is now removed from Abram's life and his God as well. Lot plays no role in the promise to those who surround Abram.

Within this interval Abraham is promised an heir despite his and Sarah's childlessness (chapter 17).[7] The narrator informs the reader that neither the adopted heir of Abraham, Eliezer, nor Ishmael (the son of Abraham and the Egyptian Hagar) will be the heir of the promise. It is appropriate that Lot is absent in this account. The man who is Abraham's relative and who accompanied him on the journey to Canaan stands outside the promise.

When the narrator next discusses Lot, the angels are visiting the corrupt city of Sodom to ascertain whether the outcry that God has heard about the place is true. The angels begin their journey at Mamre (chapter 18), and their visit to Sodom and Lot's ensuing hospitality toward them are modeled on their initial visit to Abraham at Mamre. By comparing the two stories, much can be learned about the narrator's characterization of Lot.[8]

Greeting the Visitors (Gen. 19:1-4)

When Abraham glimpsed the angels, "he ran to meet them" (*wayyārāṣ liqrǝ̄tām*, 18:2); Lot simply "got up to meet them" (*wayyāqām liqrǝ̄tām*, 19:1) without making any effort to hurry.[9] Abraham knows that any service he might wish to render to the angels must first meet their approval. He asks "Please, if I have found favor in your sight, please do not pass by your servant" (18:3). Lot, in contrast, asks that the men come to his house without any humbling statement or qualifier (19:2). Abraham's direct address to the men offers them rest and food (18:4-5) whereas the speech of Lot offers them rest alone (19:2), although the narrator later reveals in indirect discourse that a meal was prepared (19:3).[10]

The meals themselves are contrasted as well. Both Abraham and Lot prepare the meal in haste, but the one Abraham provides is more elaborate than the one Lot made. Abraham tells Sarah to take "choice flour" (*qemaḥ sōlet*) and to knead it (18:6), whereas Lot bakes unleavened bread (*maṣṣôt*, 19:3), recalling the bread made under the dire circumstances in Egypt when the Israelites fled from their enemies in haste (Exod. 12:39). Surprisingly, he does not ask either his wife or his daughters to prepare food, in contrast to Abraham's request of his wife to assist. The account at Abraham's residence describes the care with which the tender calf was prepared and tells how curds and milk were brought along with it (18:7-8). The description of the meal Lot has prepared is cursory (19:3). By reporting that the angels had not yet had the opportunity to lie down when the townspeople surround the house, the narrator effectively re-creates the haste of the meal and hints at the upcoming disaster.

The angels respond differently to Lot's and to Abraham's offers of hospitality. To Abraham they respond "Yes, do as you have said" (18:5), whereas to Lot they state starkly, "No, because we will spend the night in the street" (19:2). The angels attempt to fulfill the divine investigation without delay (18:21). Wittingly or unwittingly, Lot's suggestion that they stay with him instead of in the street has the potential to thwart the divine plan. When the angels rightly refuse, Lot "presses them strongly" *(wayyipsar-bām mĕ ʾōd,* 19:3). The verb *psr* is the same verb used when the men of Sodom press against Lot and threaten him *(wayyipsĕrû,* 19:9). The narrator's choice of this word leads the reader to ask whether Lot's actions might actually place the angels in danger.

Lot's Daughters as Substitute Victims (Gen. 19:4-11)

The drama of the angels' investigative visit crescendos when the men of the city surround Lot's house and demand to rape the angels. Faced with this threatened violence, Lot offers a violent alternative—that his daughters be raped instead. The sympathetic assessment of modern commentators regarding this action is illustrated by this statement of Bruce Vawter:

> Certainly to our tastes he [Lot] proves himself to be more sensitive to the duties of hospitality than those of fatherhood . . . the spectacle of a father offering his virgin daughters to the will and pleasure of a mob that was seeking to despoil his household would not have seemed as shocking to the ancient sense of proprieties as it may seem to us. . . . Really, there is no need to make excuses for him, as far as the biblical perspective is concerned. In all the stories about him the soundness of Lot's judgment is never the point at issue. . . . He is a good and not a bad man, but neither is he a hero in any way.[11]

John Skinner's assessment of Lot's character differs from that of Vawter, yet he also argues that although Lot's actions regarding his daughters would indeed offend the sensibilities of the people of the day, the circumstances of the mob scene excuse his behavior. He states,

> Lot's readiness to sacrifice the honour of his daughters, though abhorrent to Hebrew morality . . . shows him as a courageous champion of the obligations

of hospitality in a situation of extreme embarrassment, and is recorded to his credit.[12]

Could it be possible that the narrator believes that Lot's behavior is excusable? In a recent study, Gerda Lerner argues,

> Lot's right to dispose of his daughters, even so as to offer them to be raped, is taken for granted. It does not need to be explained; hence we can assume it reflected a historic social condition.[13]

Finding additional support with the story of the rape of the Levite's concubine (Judg. 19:22-30), Lerner concludes that these two narratives show that "the virgin daughters are as disposable as the concubine or the enslaved women captured in warfare."[14] Although it is true that this narrative shows that the daughters of Lot were, by their very status, powerless to prevent their father from abusing them, it does not necessarily follow that Lot had a right to have them raped according to the narrator. Lerner argues that the account of Lot and his daughters is a type of story that belies "practices and values which are assumed as a given and therefore remain unexplained."[15] Although such narratives may show societal practices, their mere inclusion or description does not necessarily mean that the practice was condoned or accepted. The narrator does not condone such an act merely because he or she does not expressly condemn it. The narrator may implicitly condemn Lot's action more effectively by the way he or she develops the plot than by an explicit statement. In order to glean clues to understand the view of the narrator it is necessary to examine all the literary features of the narrative about Lot. While the daughters of Lot do not figure prominently, the narrator places Lot's interactions with them in the context of the events that reveal his true character. The trajectory of Lot's life shows that he is a man who becomes quarrelsome, irresponsible, and exploitative. Just as the book of Judges incorporates the narrative of the rape of the Levite's concubine at the end of the book in order to show the increasing tendency of every man to do "what was right in his own eyes" (Judg. 21:25), so too does the narrator use the scene of the offering of Lot's daughters to comment on the situation in the city and on Lot himself.

The narrator quickly, yet dramatically, sets the scene: Lot offers sustenance and rest to the travelers, but instead they are threatened by the men of the city. The details of this most intimidating scene are chilling. The narrator states, "They had not yet lain down when the men of the city, the men of Sodom, surrounded the house—from the young to the old, all the people, down to the last" (19:4). The sentence is laden with multiple descriptions of the subject. The repeated identifications of the townsmen underscore their sheer numbers. If there were any doubt as to their numbers and strength, the final phrase answers unequivocally: the *entire* male populace demands to sexually brutalize the visitors. Lot's response is strange and shrouded in secrecy. In order to respond to the mob, he departs from the protection of his house. The narrator describes how deliberately he departed: "Lot went out of the entrance-way to the men, and shut the door after him" (*wayyēṣēʾ ʾălēhem lôṭ happethāh wĕ-haddelet sāgar ʾaḥărāyw,* 19:6). He exits to present his alternative in secret and does not elicit the assistance of his guests in thwarting the plan of the townsmen. He speaks to the men of the town as though they were comrades, addressing them as "brothers" (19:7). Inexplicably, even though Lot recognizes that their proposal is evil, he attempts to substitute another violent act.[16] The men of Sodom wanted the angels sent out by Lot's hand (*hôṣîʾēm,* 19:5); now Lot offers to send out his daughters (*ʾôṣîʾāh-nāʾ ʾethen,* 19:8), who, notably, "have not known man." The narrator dramatizes the stakes of the scene by emphasizing that Lot's daughters are virgins. Incredibly, Lot volunteers to hand them over himself and gives the crowd license to abuse them. He states, "Please let me bring them out to you so that you may do to them whatever is good in your eyes" (19:8).

It is true that Lot's callous offer is ostensibly motivated by his desire to protect his guests; however, the narrator shows that Lot is in no position to offer protection to them. In fact, the townspeople remind Lot that he, too, is a guest in Sodom, and therefore does not have the same rights as the established residents (19:9). Hospitality that protects and cares for the needs of the visitor and the stranger is an important and expected custom in the land of Israel. However, there are no indications from the Hebrew Scriptures that sexual abuse or other violence is condoned if done in the service of "hospitality."[17] As would have been known to any ancient reader of this text, sexual violence is unequivocally condemned. This is known from the accounts of the rape of Dinah and the subsequent slaughter of the Shechemites (Genesis 34), the rape and murder of the Levite's concubine (Judg. 19:22-32), the account of Tamar's ruse (Genesis 38), and the narrative of Amnon's rape of Tamar (2 Samuel 13).

In an arresting reversal, it is Lot who needs the protection of the angels. The men of the city "pressed hard against the man Lot" (19:9 RSV). They were about to break the door when the angels rescue him, bring him back into the house, which he chose to leave, and "shut the door" (19:6), which Lot had stealthily exited to offer his daughters as substitutes. Lot had shut the door (*wĕ ʾet-haddelet sāgar,* 19:6) behind him to offer his daughters to the mob. In contrast, the angels rescue Lot from the mob, bring him back to the house, "and shut the door" (*wĕ ʾet-haddelet sāgārû*, 19:10) thereby saving him.[18] The details provided by the narrator reaffirm the power of the angels and the impotence of Lot. The angels strike blind all the men at Lot's door. The men whose violent designs led them to threaten Lot by thrusting him against the door have now "exhausted themselves groping for the door" (19:11). They are eviscerated not by Lot's pleading but by the angels' action. Any doubts the reader may have had about the wickedness of Sodom are quickly dissipated. The previous events described make it clear that all the men of the town are wicked. Lot's offer of his daughters demonstrates that his actions are questionable also.

The scene concludes with the angels, Lot, and his daughters safe, and the townsmen blind. It should be apparent to Lot that these men are actually angels from God. Yet except for an introductory phrase that informs the reader that the visitors are angels (19:1), the narrator does not use the term "angels" (*hammalʾākîm*) again until verse 15 in order to underscore Lot's inability to recognize them.

Exiting the City (Gen. 19:12-29)

In spite of his rescue by the angels, Lot continues to demonstrate moral blindness. Clearly, all the men of the town are wicked, and because of Lot's behavior, he, too, is under suspicion. The angels have no other choice but to destroy the city.

The angels specifically tell Lot to save his (future) sons-in-law, daughters, and anyone else in his household by leaving Sodom. The term used to refer to the sons-in-law, *ḥātān*, can also be translated "future son-in-law" or "bridegroom." It is best to conclude that the narrator wants the reader to assume that these men are the betrothed of Lot's virgin daughters since no other wives are indicated. Lot has acted cruelly by offering his daughters to the men of the city, and he also commits a crime against these (future) sons-in-law.[19]

Instead of obeying the angels' command, Lot continues to falter. He does not act; he speaks—not to everyone, but to the sons-in-law alone. He ignores his own daughters, even though the angels specifically command him to save them. Unlike the angels, he gives no reason when he tells the sons-in-law about God's plan to destroy Sodom. The sons-in-law conclude Lot is jesting. The narrator is ambiguous as to whether the misunderstanding is their fault or Lot's because of his manner of presentation. In either case the reader knows that Lot fails to gather his entire family and take them out without delay as instructed.[20]

Inexplicably, Lot ignores the other warnings of the angels. In spite of the angels' urgency, Lot does not lead his family out as commanded even by the following morning. The angels instruct him again to take his wife and daughters out to escape the punishment. Failure to mention the sons-in-law may be the narrator's way of suggesting that they left after Lot initially approached them. Yet again Lot delays (19:16). The angels must seize him and his family to bring them out. In spite of Lot's obstinacy they are rescued because of "YHWH being merciful to him" (19:16).

Lot's appreciation of the severity of the situation does not improve even after the initial rescue. The narrator dramatically records the angels' instructions to Lot, commands that are given to him alone. Twice he is told to flee (*himmālēṭ*), without stopping or looking back. Yet Lot does not flee (19:17). The play on words between "Lot" (*lôṭ*) and "flee" (*himmālēṭ*) heightens the irony of his obstinacy.[21] Presuming he finds favor in the angels' sight (19:19), he protests and assumes that his opinions are superior to the angels' commands. Concluding that obeying them might mean his death, he pleads to flee to a little city instead of to the hills. The mercy shown to Lot continues and he is told that this wish will be granted, in spite of the fact that the city, Zoar, was apparently marked for destruction as well. After Lot's plea one of the angels agrees not to overthrow that city (19:21). Although the angel instructs Lot to go in haste, Lot does not arrive there until the following day (19:23, cf. 19:15). He thus delays even though the city is "close enough to flee to" (19:20). The narrator concludes by drawing more attention to Lot's inability to obey the angels' commands quickly and precisely.

Lot's mistreatment of his family (first his daughters, then his sons-in-law) continues. Lot's wife looks back, indicating her desire to return to the city, and turns into a pillar of salt despite the angels' warning to Lot. The narrator provides a gap that prompts the reader to ask whether it would have been likely for Lot to have informed his wife. Given his previous behavior, the reader is led to conclude that Lot probably remained silent.

Lot is portrayed as an insincere, self-centered individual who is disrespectful to God's angels, exploits his daughters' welfare, and is a procrastinating dweller in a sinful city. Why, then, was he saved from Sodom? The answer comes from the omniscient narrator's description of God's perspective. "God remembered Abraham" and "sent Lot out of the midst of the overthrow" (19:29 RSV). It is because of Lot's connection with

39

Abraham, not because of his own righteousness, that he is spared. The narrator has made a powerful statement by placing the tradition of the angels' visit to Lot in Sodom immediately after Abraham's questioning of God's justice (chapter 18). In fact, Genesis 18 leaves the reader with crucial questions. Are there ten righteous men in Sodom? And if there are fewer than ten, will even these innocents suffer? Both questions are answered in chapter 19. There are not ten righteous men in Sodom. In fact, there are none. Even Lot is seriously flawed. He offers to substitute an attack on his daughters for an assault on his guests; he presumes he finds favor in God's sight, yet he tarries and delays when commanded to leave. He does not lead his family out of the city and jeopardizes his daughters' well-being after the departure. Clearly he is not portrayed sympathetically.

Lot's Care for his Daughters (Gen. 19:30-38)

The story of Lot does not end with the destruction of Sodom and Gomorrah. The last account of this man concerns an incestuous union with his daughters. Through this union he becomes the progenitor of the two groups of people who are the enemies of Israel. Vawter argues that "this story, tenuously connected with the preceding narrative, obviously had little to do with the Sodom and Gomorrah saga and owes its preservation to other concerns."[22] On the contrary, the narrator already connects this account by the geographic references to Zoar and to the hills that played a crucial role in understanding Lot's actions in the Sodom and Gomorrah story. Moreover, the daughters' sexuality was important in the beginning of the Sodom and Gomorrah narrative and it now comes up again. The narrator shows that Lot's irresponsible actions continue to lead to disaster.

The choice of the place where Lot settles is surprising. Although he had insisted on going to Zoar instead of to the hills, as the angels commanded, he apparently becomes afraid to remain there and goes to dwell in the hills after all. The narrator provides adequate information to conclude that Lot has been neither a good provider nor a protector of his unmarried daughters.[23] The daughters, who were once betrothed, now are without hope of finding husbands in the remote hills.[24] They live in difficult conditions: they dwell in a cave (19:30).[25] The term "cave" (*mĕ'ārāh*) is used throughout the Hebrew Bible to indicate a hiding place, place of refuge in time of trouble, or a burial place.[26] In these circumstances there is no possibility that they could obtain husbands since they are isolated as well as impoverished.

These women, who have been passive throughout the narrative, now take action; they cleverly plan to obtain the means for changing their powerless existence. For the first time one of them speaks. The eldest daughter explains her plan to the younger: "Our father is old and there is no man on earth to come into us as is the custom of all the earth. Come, let us make our father drink wine and let us lie with him so that we will preserve life by our father's seed" (19:31-32). In her isolation she fears that they are the only ones left on earth. Her desire to "preserve life" (*ŭněhayyeh*) from Lot's seed recalls God's command to Noah that animals must be taken into the ark so that "seed might live" (*lěhayyôt*, 7:3). The narrator makes clear that their dire circumstances prompt them to act for understandable reasons.

While it is true that the daughters scheme to make their father drink wine so that they can become pregnant by him, Lot irresponsibly becomes so drunk on two separate occasions that when each daughter had sexual relations with him, "He did not know when she lay down or when she arose" (19:33, 35 RSV). Lot is pathetic—he does not even know what has happened to him. Up to this point, Lot has threatened and neglected them. Only when intoxicated does he finally provide for his daughters. In a reversal of justice, the man who offered to have his daughters sexually brutalized is now manipulated sexually.[27] The daughters' actions achieve the intended results—both become pregnant. The daughters continue to act resolutely when their children are born. They, not Lot, name them; in fact, Lot does not appear again. Even in his absence, however, Lot's legacy continues in his offspring. The eldest daughter names her son Moab, and the younger names her son ben-Ami, names that point to Lot as the progenitor in popular Hebrew etymology. The Septuagint additions to the Hebrew text provide clues to the popular understanding. The Septuagint adds the phrase, "saying, from my father," to explain the eldest daughter's naming of her son Moab and the phrase, "the son of my family," to comment on the younger daughter's choice of the name ben-Ami.

All the incidents in Genesis that deal with Lot clearly indicate that he continually puts himself and others at risk either deliberately or unwittingly. He is self-centered in his land-dealing with Abraham; he dwells in a region known for its iniquity; he risks Abraham's life when he is captured. Lot is incompetent in protecting his guests; he risks his daughters' lives and welfare. He disobeys the commands from the angels to depart from Sodom. He ends his days as a destitute father of two unmarried daughters by whom he fathers two peoples who will continually be at strife with Israel. In contrast to past studies, this interpretation of the Lot cycle indicates that the narrator intends to demonstrate that Lot becomes increasingly estranged from Abraham and the covenantal promises associated with him. Lot's behavior with his daughters is inexcusable. His treatment of his daughters is not an isolated act but is one of many dubious actions.[28]

In contrast to their father, the daughters of Lot lack the privileges Lot enjoyed while accompanying Abraham. Lot's circumstances seem to indicate that he will control his own destiny. Yet each choice he makes brings him farther away from Abraham and the promises made to him by God. Unexpectedly, the daughters who were to be abused and who live isolated, destitute lives shape the destinies of three peoples: the Ammonites, Moabites, and Israelites. The Israelites must live alongside their direct descendants and continually compete and fight them. The daughters' own hardships are reflected in the contentiousness of their peoples. Like the descendants of Hagar, these two peoples are related to the Israelites. Lot was the nephew of Abraham, yet their lives diverge. The narrator shows that the origins of these two enemy people are shameful—through incest. But the recognition that they are related reveals an understanding of the interconnectedness of peoples in spite of their political contentions.

4

Hagar

Powerless
Foreigner

When driven by suffering and disappointment, individuals frequently turn to others for help in solving their difficulties. In such circumstances, persons of prestige, wealth, and education have more resources than do people who are poor, uneducated, or foreign-born. Persons of means are more likely to be in a position to elicit the assistance of others who may become reluctant participants in their dramas. Either law or circumstances may prevent those pressed into service from asserting their right to refuse. At times the forcefulness of such situations is obvious—a master might use a slave, a parent might turn to a dependent child—but at other times the power that one holds over another human being is perhaps more subtle. For example, one's education, situation at birth, income, and prestige of employment, as well as race, sex, and marital status, all contribute to the way society values and therefore treats a person and in turn how that person may respond. When the poor or disadvantaged are used by the wealthy or advantaged, they often lack the power and resources to find redress. It may be impossible to escape the demands of others, no matter how noble those demands seem to be.

The story of Hagar is a portrayal of a woman who has little control over her destiny and therefore is required to do the bidding of her mistress. A foreigner in the land of Canaan, she lives as a servant in the household of two other newcomers to the land, Abram and Sarai. As the years pass and Sarai remains childless, she looks to Hagar as the solution to her infertility. Hagar is powerless to object and becomes the secondary wife to a man who impregnates her at his first wife's request. The plan goes awry, however, and Hagar suffers because of Sarai's jealousy. Forced out of the household and driven to the threshold of death, this woman who has no advocate is addressed by God.

Introduction to Hagar (Gen. 16:1-6)

This introductory narrative was examined closely in the discussion of Sarai;[1] thus its importance needs only be pointed out for Hagar's story. Hagar is introduced not as a person in her own right, but as the maidservant of Sarai, who sees her as a solution to her own trauma of childlessness. When introduced, Hagar is an unmarried, childless woman, who serves Sarai, a woman who is also childless. Yet their respective stations in life separate these two women. Sarai is a married woman and Hagar is a servant. Little information is given about Hagar. Identified as an Egyptian servant, the narrator suggests that Abram obtained Hagar when he and Sarai were in Egypt.[2] Although the root etymology of her name is unknown, its similarity in sound to *haggēr* ("sojourner/newcomer/temporary dweller") appropriately connotes her role in the lives of the first ancestors of Israel, Abram and Sarai.[3]

Having escaped the threat from Pharaoh, Sarai unwittingly sets herself up for an additional threat from another Egyptian—a woman she did not expect to cause her difficulty—the powerless Hagar. Compelled by her continuing inability to have a child, Sarai tells Abram to have sex with Hagar. By this union, Hagar becomes Abram's secondary wife or concubine.[4] As was discussed earlier, having a child by a surrogate mother was not unusual.[5] Although it is possible that the narrator wants the reader to believe that Hagar considered this demand demeaning to her, it is more likely that the narrator suggests that initially she considered her relationship with Abram to be an elevation of her status.[6] The narrator never uses Hagar's own words or gives her own perspective, thereby creating a gap in the reader's understanding that must be kept in abeyance as the narrative continues. At the same time, Hagar's silence may be contrasted with Sarai's determination to do something about her infertility.

Hagar is not the only character who remains silent in this scene. Abram, too, remains silent when confronted by Sarai. In this way, the narrator emphasizes Abram's lack of interest in her plight.[7] In the meantime, the same act that underscores Hagar's powerlessness concomitantly becomes an opportunity for Hagar to experience the first act of power she

44

has over Sarai. Hagar now has something that Sarai is desperate for—the required sexual union with Abram has resulted in her pregnancy. The narrator gives us a glimpse of what Hagar's pregnancy means to her. She senses her increased status over Sarai; Sarai thereby becomes an object of her contempt, and Hagar makes her feelings known to her mistress.[8] Sarai senses, even before Hagar's child is born, that her plan has failed. Hagar shows no intentions of releasing her child to be considered the child of Sarai.[9] Indeed, it is ironic that Hagar is an Egyptian and that Sarah attempts to preserve her own family line through a woman whose own people later threaten the Israelites. As the text relates, it is not only the Egyptians who will pose a threat to Israel, but so too will the descendants of Hagar.

The absence of Hagar's response to becoming Abram's secondary wife enables the narrator to present the truly ambiguous nature of her status. What would normally be an elevation in her social standing and that which initially gives her a sense of power over Sarai actually becomes an occasion that lowers her standing. She moves from being a servant in the household of Sarai to being homeless. Sarai maltreats her, Abram abdicates any responsibility, and thus this pregnant woman must flee from the only home she knows. Pregnant and forced to flee, the narrator shows that she faces her suffering alone. In a dramatic reversal, however, God will address her in the wilderness to which she flees.

Hagar's Encounter with the Messenger of God on the Road to Shur (Gen. 16:7-12)

The narrator hints at Hagar's destiny and legacy by identifying the location of her encounter with the messenger of God at the well on the road to Shur. Located beyond the eastern border of Egypt, Shur is first mentioned here in the Hebrew Bible. It becomes one of the dwelling places of her son Ishmael (25:18). Moreover, Hagar's descendants here will be in conflict with the descendants of Sarai; indeed, Saul and David later struggle with the people of these territories (1 Sam. 15:7; 27:8). Not only is this geographic location significant, but so too is the location at the well. By including this reference, the narrator indicates that although Hagar is in barren territory, she is at a life-giving source. It is precisely at this well where a messenger, or angel, of the God of Israel speaks to this Egyptian woman.[10]

The message given to Hagar contains both heartening and disquieting news. The twofold nature of the message is suggested first by the way in which the angel speaks to her: she is identified as the "servant of Sarai."[11]

The importance of this identification becomes apparent when she is told to continue in this role. Hagar's first words in the narrative underscore her own suffering. In responding to the messenger she states, "From Sarai, my mistress, I am fleeing" (16:8). Her suffering is also indicated by the narrator's placement of the angel's word to her. Although the messenger has both a difficult and a hopeful message, the painful message is given first. Immediately after Hagar identifies the source of her suffering, the angel tells her, "Return to your mistress, and humble yourself under her hand" (16:9). The word used for "humble yourself" *(hit'annî)* recalls the description of the harsh treatment that Sarai had inflicted upon her earlier *(te'annehā,* 16:6), and the narrator thus indicates that Hagar's pain at the hands of Sarai will not be abated.

The message, however, is not completely bleak. Hagar is given the promise that her descendants will be multiplied innumerably. While it is true that the promise given to her is not put in a covenantal context, it nonetheless recalls the promises given to Abraham to become a great nation (13:16, 17:2, 22:17) and clearly is viewed by the narrator as being positive.[12] Thus, the messenger assures Hagar directly that "YHWH has heard about your suffering" (16:11). By placing this promise in the context of divine assurance, the narrator indicates that God assuages Hagar's suffering by promising that her offspring will be a great nation. Hagar is told by the angel to name her child "Ishmael," meaning "God hears," thus recalling God's involvement in Hagar's affliction and Ishmael's birth. The conflict between Hagar and Sarai will not end with their generation, however, but will continue with their descendants.[13] This struggle is already indicated by the description of Hagar's son who will be "a wild ass of a man" (16:12). The term "wild ass" *(pere')* is used throughout the Hebrew Bible to indicate stubbornness, idolatry, and lack of refinement.[14] This term not only indicates the strength of the descendants of Hagar as they confront the children of Sarah, but also their low status in the eyes of the Israelites.[15]

Aftermath of the Encounter (Gen. 16:13-16)

The narrator heightens the impact of Hagar's encounter with the angel by permitting the reader to experience it through Hagar's words. The text reads: "And she called the name of YHWH who spoke to her, 'You are God of Seeing' because she explained, 'Yet here have I seen after the one who sees me?' " (16:13). Although the Hebrew of this phrase is difficult, it is clear that Hagar has named the Deity in response to her experience. God has seen her, the experience did not consume her, and she still lives to receive God's plan for her and for her child.[16] The narrator indicates that Hagar appropriated this experience and identified it by her unique naming of God. Throughout the Hebrew Bible, the appellations of God are either given by the Deity itself or by a person who has experienced a revelation. By recording Hagar's actions, the narrator has demonstrated that the God of Israel responds to a foreigner, is revealed to her, and is appropriately named by her. In addition, Hagar's naming of God—"God of Seeing"—and the revelation itself have a permanent legacy for the people who live in the area of the well. It becomes known as Beerlahairoi—the Well of the One Who Lives and Sees Me.

Hagar's return journey to the household of Sarai is neither related nor commented upon directly by the narrator, but it is arresting to note that the descriptions provided of her life back in the household of Abram and Sarai refer only to encounters with Abram. The narrator relates that "Abram called the name of his son, whom Hagar bore, Ishmael." Some commentators see the naming by Abram as a displacement of the role promised to Hagar by God, namely, that *she* would name the child. It is also possible, however, that the narrator is showing that Abram abided by Hagar's naming and instructions.

As the account closes there is still no mention of Sarai. The narrator thus creates a temporary gap that prompts the reader to ask: How did Sarai treat Hagar? How did Sarai respond to the son of Hagar and Abram? How, in turn, does Hagar relate to Sarai? Indeed, the next scene with Hagar shows that this silence belies great tension. Meanwhile, the reader's attention is drawn to other issues that are important for understanding the full impact of the birth of Hagar's son.

The Interim Scenes (Gen. 17–20)

The final note given in the first narrative about Hagar indicates that Abram was 86 years old when Ishmael was born (16:16). When we next encounter Hagar, Abram is 100 years old. In the 14 intervening years, much has taken place that will set the stage for Hagar's final encounter with Sarai and Abram. The structure of the narrative indicates that there are three important events: God's promise to both Abram and Sarai of a son, the rupture between Abram and Lot, and the threat to Sarai from Abimelech. All three exigencies emphasize the fragility of the origins of the Israelites.

In chapters 17 and 18, God specifies for the first time that the promise to Abram for a son will come from the birth of a child to the aged Sarai. Indeed, Abraham and Sarah's names are changed as an indication of this fact.[17] Intertwined with this promise, however, is God's revelation to Abraham that Ishmael will also be the recipient of a promise although it will not include a covenant. For the first time, Abraham learns of God's plan for Ishmael. Recalling the words of the angel of God to Hagar, who told Hagar that God "heard" (paid heed to) her suffering (šāmaʿ, 16:11), the narrator states that God said to Abraham, "I have heard you" (šĕmaʿtî hā, 17:20). The promise to Abraham and Sarah is fragile not only because of the couple's age, but because the firstborn son of Abraham, Ishmael, also receives a promise.

In chapters 18 and 19, the narrator shows that there is another person associated with Abraham who will also be cut off from the nascent Israelite community, and who, like Hagar, will be the progenitor of a rival people. Lot, who is estranged from Abraham, nevertheless is rescued on account of him, just as Ishmael is saved not only because God hears Hagar's affliction (chapter 16) but also because God hears Abraham's pleading for him (chapter 18). However, Lot's journey to Canaan with Abraham and Sarah takes a surprising turn. Through an incestuous relationship with his daughters, he becomes the father of the Ammonites and Moabites, two peoples who will contend with the Israelites throughout their history. Like the Ishmaelites, these peoples come into existence before Isaac is born.

The final interim account (chapter 20) relates that the future birth of a child to Abraham and Sarah is precarious not only because of the age of the couple and the advent of rival nations, but also because of threats to the mother of the yet unborn child. Because Sarah was taken into Abimelech's harem, the father of her child could have been a man other than Abraham. Due to God's intervention, however, Sarah was never sexually approached.[18]

These accounts are framed by the two narratives of Hagar's experiences. The first narrative concerning Hagar shows how the Ishmaelite people were born—through a rivalry between two women, one who suffered because of her debilitating childlessness, the other because of the abuse she experienced in her powerlessness. The account is indicative of the narrator's attitude toward descendants of Ishmael. They come into existence because of Sarah's frustration and are heard by God, even if they are not given a covenant. In addition, they are not presented as being completely different from the Israelite people themselves because they share the same father. The Israelites similarly are related to other rival peoples, the Ammonites and Moabites, because their father Lot was the nephew of Abraham. The precariousness of Israelite existence is shown not only by Hagar's implicit threat to Sarah, but also by the overt threat from Abimelech. The second narrative concerning Hagar shows that the rivalries between the descendants of Sarah and the descendants of Hagar escalate and are not permanently resolved.

The Birth of Isaac and the Escalation of the Rivalry (Gen. 21:1-13)

The continuing rivalry between Sarah and Hagar was examined in chapter 2.[19] After the birth of Isaac, Sarah fears Hagar and her son and commands that Abraham cast them out. Abraham discovers that God sanctions Sarah's demand, and for the third time, God promises that the son of Hagar will be the progenitor of a nation.

Hagar's Journey into Despair (Gen. 21:14-16)

For the second time in her experience, Hagar is driven from the household of Sarah. This time she does not leave on account of her own desperation but is forced out by Abraham.[20] When Abraham sends Hagar and Ishmael away, he follows both the command of Sarah and of God. Although the reader at first may fear that God has abandoned Hagar to Sarah's fears, it must be remembered that God has reiterated the promise that Hagar's son will prosper (21:13). Nonetheless, the narrator is sensitive to Hagar's plight. Abraham waits until the next day to send her away and gives her provisions for the journey, but the harshness of the territory and the paucity of the food and water are also described. More arresting is the narrator's description of Hagar on this journey; she "wandered about (*watēta*ᶜ) in the wilderness of Beersheba" (21:14). This word connotes the pain of displacement and disorientation.[21] It is appropriate to find Hagar in this frontier territory of Beersheba, the southern limits of the land that will become Israel, because her descendants will be found on the outskirts of this region. The reference thereby points to the fact that Hagar's descendants indeed have a future.

Hagar's suffering continues. Whereas in her first experience of exile she found herself at a well, here she is in the wilderness with a container of water that soon becomes empty. The narrator underscores her plight by the description of the place where she leaves her child—"under one of the bushes" (21:15). Although the narrator could have used another word for bush (such as *sĕneh*), the one chosen, *śîaḥ*, is especially appropriate because its homonym, *śîaḥ*, means "complaint" or "lamentation."[22] In describing

Hagar's despair, however, the narrator also hints at God's forthcoming response to her lament. Hagar puts the child at a distance from her to be spared the sight of his death. The space between them is described literally as "making distant like shooters of a bow," that is, "a bowshot off" (21:16). This expression is singularly attested to in the Hebrew Scriptures. The reference to the bow *(qešet)* is proleptic of the description that Ishmael will become known as an excellent bowman. Hagar's lament and despair contrast with her earlier experience of God in the wilderness. As opposed to her proclamation that she had witnessed the God of Seeing (16:13), she now states that she cannot look at *(ʾerʾeh)* the death of her child. The narrator strikes a sympathetic chord for Hagar by allowing us to experience the poignancy of this scene from her perspective. The narrator relates that "she lifted up her voice and wept" (21:16).

God's Response (Gen. 21:17-19)

At the point of Hagar's deepest suffering, the narrator shows that God responds to the dying child. Upon hearing the voice of the child God responds and a messenger of God appears to Hagar. At first reading, it may appear that God is concerned only for the child and not for Hagar because the narrator states that God heard the boy's voice and not her own.[23] However, Hagar is crying because her child is dying; by hearing the cry of the boy, God is responding to the imminent death of the child, which, of course, causes Hagar to weep. Moreover, the messenger specifically addresses Hagar. Unlike her earlier encounter, this time she is addressed by her own name, without the appositive "servant of Sarah." The message to Hagar is one of consolation. She is told neither to be troubled nor to fear.

God reiterates the promise about Ishmael given first to Hagar when she was pregnant and fleeing from Sarai: "I will establish him a great nation" (21:18). Although the promise is given to her son, and not directly to her, the narrator does not interpret this as God's neglect of Hagar. Rather, Hagar resembles the wives of the patriarchs who give birth to sons and who participate in the lives of their families in important and independent ways in order to fulfill God's plan for their people.[24]

Hagar will be involved in strengthening her son for his role as the progenitor of an important nation. Indeed, the God that Hagar had named at the well on the road to Shur, "the God of Seeing," now "opened her eyes, and she saw *(wattēreʾ)* a well of water" (21:19). Just as God addresses the needs of her dying son first, Hagar, too, gives drink to him upon seeing this well. The narrator indicates that God is committed to strengthening Hagar's child by the choice of referents for him. Throughout chapter 21, the name "Ishmael" does not appear—he is referred to either as "the son of the slave woman" (by Sarah), or as "the child" *(yeled),* or as "the youth" *(naʿar).* The term *yeled* most often is used of a newborn or young child, and although *naʿar* sometimes can refer to an infant, it is more commonly used to indicate a youth about to enter adulthood.[25] God always refers to Ishmael as "the youth" (21:11, 17, 18, 20), as does the narrator in describing Hagar's response to her son after the revelation; but Hagar refers to him as "the child," as does the narrator in describing events that occur before God's intervention (21:14, 15, 16). After Ishmael is saved by the drink from the well, the narrator uses the term "youth" even when referring to Hagar's actions toward him (21:19). By restricting the use of the term "child" to refer to Ishmael when his life is threatened in the desert, the narrator underscores his weakness and suffering. However, as God revealed to Abraham (21:12), Ishmael lives and fathers a great nation; thus in these instances the term "youth" is used to emphasize his strength. Similarly, in order to acknowledge God's hand in protecting and saving Ishmael, the narrator, too, uses the term "youth," even to describe Hagar's actions with him once the crisis has passed.[26] The frightening desert experience has now become the locus of another encounter between Hagar and God.

The Continuing Story of Hagar and Her Son (Gen. 21:20-21)

The narrator shows that God's involvement with Hagar and her son is not limited to times of crisis. The narrator states, "God was with the youth while he grew up" (21:20). Ishmael's experience in the desert continues to influence his life; not only is God with him, but he grows up to be "a bowman" *(rōbeh qaššāt),* recalling the description of his imminent death in the desert, when Hagar placed him "a bowshot away." The narrator identifies the place where he lives as the region of Paran, which is in the vicinity of the wilderness of Shur, where Hagar first fled. This area, crossed by Israel when fleeing from the Egyptians during the Exodus, becomes the region in which the descendants of Hagar the Egyptian will flourish.

In contrast to the events in Hagar's life with Abraham and Sarah that emphasized her powerlessness, Hagar's final action is one of strength. She continues to have a role in the development of her son, as God commanded her in the wilderness. Hagar is the only woman in the Bible to choose a wife for her son. By choosing a woman from Egypt, she ensures the continuation of her traditions, culture, and values. Ishmael is related to Isaac by their father, but his mother has ensured the Egyptian character of her descendants. We do not hear about Hagar again, but we do learn that Ishmael lives a long life and has twelve sons (25:12-18), thus ensuring a multitude of descendants. By this description, the narrator shows that Ishmael's destiny is parallel to that of Jacob.

Conclusions

Throughout Hagar's life she experiences estrangement as a foreigner, hardship as a servant, grief as an abandoned pregnant woman, and the despair of two occasions when she must face her own imminent death and the death of her child. In spite of these difficulties, Hagar responds to the God who addresses her. Although she is never able to demand redress from Sarah and Abraham for abandoning her, she does live her remaining years as an independent woman who chooses one of her own people for her son's wife. The narrator clearly indicates, by listing her many descendants, that Hagar's legacy is vast. The narrator uses Hagar's story to relate that the tension that exists between Sarah's descendants and Hagar's descendants is rooted in the births of these two peoples. By placing these troubles at the birth of the peoples' respective progenitors, the narrator has underscored their tenacity. At the same time, the narrator does not present a caricature of Hagar or her descendants. The narrator speaks both of Sarah's desperation to have a child as well as of Hagar's contempt for Sarah and Sarah's exploitative response. Hagar's plight as a woman facing destitution and death is sensitively portrayed, and the narrator does not hesitate to show that God twice responds to her. Perhaps God's promise to Hagar to make Ishmael the father of a great nation may not impress some as enough of a personal vindication, but for a powerless woman of her culture, it is a striking reward.

5

Rebekah

The Decisive
Matriarch

In many societies women's accomplishments have gone unrecognized, and women are valued only for the pleasure they give or for the work they complete for those in power. Thus represented, their full range of achievements can be dismissed, ignored, or underestimated. A stereotyped view of a more primitive age might suggest that the Israelites would write only a schematic or undeveloped portrait of Rebekah. However, rather than minimizing Rebekah's contribution to the Israelite people, the narratives that introduce and develop the portrait of the second of the matriarchs are striking in the way in which she is depicted. Although she is described as being a beautiful wife for Isaac, she is not appreciated solely for her appearance. Like Abraham, her independence and trust are demonstrated by her willingness to leave her family and travel to a strange land. Not only is she the mother of the twins Esau and Jacob, but she ensures that God's designated choice, Jacob, the second-born, receives Isaac's blessing. Thus, Rebekah assists in the fulfillment of the covenantal promise of land, descendants, and blessing to the future generations of her people.

The interpretation of the Rebekah cycle of stories by biblical scholars has not been as favorable to her as is the biblical text itself. Her active role in God's plan has been either ignored or disparaged by modern commentators. She has been portrayed as either an obedient vessel or a scheming wife. Although interpreters often examine the individual patriarchs (Abraham, Isaac, and Jacob), Rebekah is usually viewed only as a part of the

Isaac cycle of stories, or as Isaac's wife. However, not all the narratives about Rebekah include Isaac; significantly, some narratives that concern Rebekah present her as an important character in her own right. This chapter examines all of the texts in Genesis that feature Rebekah. The events in these accounts, the use of dialogue, narration, passage of time, and other literary features provide clues that demonstrate how she was regarded in Israel. Not only will the relevance of each narrative be considered, but each will be examined in its context. This twofold investigation will provide a more accurate assessment of the narratives about her.

The Genealogy of Rebekah (Gen. 22:20-24)

The introduction to the name of Rebekah and her family origins is not dramatically presented; her name is found in a genealogical list. Genealogies call for special attention, however, as they indicate important links between peoples. This particular genealogy identifies the closest relatives of Abraham; among them is Rebekah, who is as yet unknown. Because the narrator identifies her as a member of Abraham's family, the reader is prompted to consider whether she, too, might participate in the covenantal relationship with God. Indeed, her name is strategically placed in a context that emphasizes her importance.

This genealogy presents the names of the children born to Abraham's brother Nahor and his sister-in-law Milcah. Nahor and Milcah's eight sons are listed, but the offspring of these eight sons, the third generation, are mentioned in only two cases. The offspring of Kemuel and Bethuel alone are deemed significant. The name of Kemuel's son, Aram, is given only in a parenthetical phrase. In contrast, Bethuel's offspring is given greater attention. A separate phrase announces, "Bethuel begat Rebekah" (22:23). Moreover, her name is arresting in this context because she is the first female offspring who is mentioned. This genealogy signifies that Rebekah, the daughter of Bethuel, ultimately comes from the union of Nahor and Milcah, the wife of the higher status, and not from the union of Nahor and his concubine. Those descendants are listed only after the announcement of Rebekah in the same genealogical list (22:24).[1]

The narrator's placement of this genealogy after the account of the testing of Abraham with his son Isaac (22:1-19) emphasizes the importance of Rebekah. In that account, God told Abraham to sacrifice his son Isaac, but later rescinded the command. As the account of Abraham's obedience comes to a close, the reader is comforted to know that Isaac has not been sacrificed and is assured that the promise of God to Abraham for descendants

54

has not been thwarted. Nonetheless, Isaac is not married and there are as yet no apparent possibilities of his opportunity to father any children. When Rebekah's name is first mentioned in the genealogy, it is not yet determined that she is a marriage candidate for Isaac. However, shortly after her name is given the reader learns that Abraham arranges for Isaac to obtain a wife from Abraham's ancestral home. Might Rebekah be God's destined one for Isaac? The placement of the genealogy of Rebekah after the account of Abraham's testing subtly indicates a hopeful future for Isaac.

The Introduction of Rebekah (Genesis 24:1-61)

The narrator first introduces Rebekah as a young woman of marriageable age. Abraham sends his servant back to his homeland to find a suitable woman for Isaac. Concerned that Isaac might marry a foreigner or that Isaac might move away from the promised land to marry, Abraham explains in detail the background and qualities of the yet unknown woman. As the servant meets and learns about Rebekah and her family, all the desired characteristics unfold.[2]

In investigating Abraham's instructions to his servant it is important to note that the narrator places this account following the information that relates that Sarah is already dead (23:2).[3] In spite of Sarah's struggles with her servant Hagar and her being at risk with Pharaoh and with Abimelech, she was able to fulfill her destined task as one of the seven ancestors of the people of Israel.[4] The question to be considered at this point is the identity and role of the mother of the next generation. Not only has Sarah died, but as the account of Abraham's instructions begins, we read that he "was old, advanced in days" (24:1).[5] By emphasizing Abraham's age, the narrator reminds the reader that he, too, is approaching death. The future of God's promise of descendants must rest with Isaac and his wife. Indeed, at this point in the Book of Genesis, the narratives about Abraham and Sarah have ended and the focus shifts to the second generation. The figure of Abraham without Sarah continues here transitionally. The promise no longer rests with Abraham and Sarah, but now must be continued with Isaac and Rebekah. Will God's promise of descendants be continued?

Besides informing us that Abraham is aged, the narrator begins the account in chapter 24 by reminding the reader that God "had blessed Abraham in everything" (24:1). As the focus turns to Isaac, the reader must consider how the blessing will continue with him. Abraham begins the proceedings to obtain a wife for Isaac from among his own kin. The narrator gives no explicit reason why Abraham does not send Isaac himself to find his wife in Haran. This absence of information prompts us to consider the danger of the long journey from Canaan to Abraham and Sarah's ancestral home. Is it possible that Abraham wanted to protect his son from danger? The narrator has previously shown that Isaac was at risk when Abraham was tested by God, but the text does not yield any definitive answers. Nonetheless, because Isaac himself does not attend to this crucial task, a greater degree of uncertainty is prompted by the account. Surely it will be more difficult for the woman's family to give permission for her to leave and for the woman herself to agree to travel to Canaan to marry a man who is not himself present. By introducing these gaps, the narrator suggests that God's providential care for the continuation of the Israelites is paramount.

Before the narrator introduces Rebekah, the reader's attention is drawn to the servant whom Abraham sends to find Isaac a wife. It is striking that Isaac is not sent. Abraham's reluctance to have his son leave Canaan points to the precarious nature of the promises of land and descendants. In spite of Isaac's absence from this crucial journey, the seriousness of the mission remains preeminent because Abraham selects the oldest and most experienced servant of the household to journey to Haran. The reason for the journey, namely, the continuation of Abraham's progeny through Isaac, is suggested from the beginning by the oath the servant must take: the servant must put his hand under Abraham's thigh. Although the full significance of this type of oath is not known, it seems to imply dire consequences to the one taking the oath if it is not fulfilled.[6] The seriousness of the oath and potential difficulties in fulfilling it are stressed by the servant's delay in responding. Instead of immediately agreeing to Abraham's request, the pace of the narrative slows and the servant raises an important objection. It is crucial to notice exactly what the servant sees as a potential impediment to the fulfillment of Abraham's command; when he later retells this account, he makes some alterations.

First, he asks Abraham whether he may take Isaac to the woman if she refuses to accompany him back to Canaan. He states to Abraham, ''Perhaps the woman may not be willing to come with me to this land; should I have your son dwell in the land that you left?'' (24:5). The seriousness of the promise of land as well as progeny becomes evident in Abraham's response. Because the narrator uses Abraham's direct speech, there can be no question as to the content of his commands. In a lengthy explanation, Abraham passionately relates in detail that the land coupled with the promise of descendants is part of God's covenantal promise. Twice the servant is told that under no circumstances is Isaac to be brought out of the land (24:6, 8). Only if the woman refuses to go will the servant be freed from the oath. Abraham concedes, "But if the woman is not willing to come with you, then you will be free from this oath of mine; only you must not have my son dwell there" (24:8). Note that Abraham assumes the woman will have the final say in the matter.

As this scene ends the reader is encouraged to consider several questions. Will the servant be successful in finding the appropriate woman? Will the woman's family approve of the marriage? Will she herself consent? Will she return safely with the servant? Will Isaac approve? As the scene shifts to the departure of the servant, the first question is considered. The servant departs well equipped. Ten camels and various gifts put him in an advantageous position to convince the future bride and her family that his master indeed has been blessed.[7]

It is clear that the encounter of the servant and Rebekah at the well is a type-scene where the hero meets the future betrothed at a well.[8] Other such type-scenes occur in Gen. 29:1-14, where Jacob meets Rachel, and in Exod. 2:15-21, where Moses encounters Zipporah. However, in this instance the absence of Isaac heightens the suspense of the outcome. Some commentators judge the meeting to be one that proceeds without difficulty or suspense. However, a close reading of the text shows that the narrator uses dialogue and ambiguity to cast doubt on the outcome of the encounter and on the servant's success. It is not simply whether or not God watches over the servant, as Abraham indicated (24:7) would occur. Rather, in reading this narrative, the servant's words and actions must be carefully noted.

The servant begins with the appropriate attitude when he undertakes this journey and addresses "YHWH God of Abraham," and reminds God of the past faithfulness to his master Abraham (24:12). The narrator's arrangement of the servant's prayer before his asking for a sign initially encourages the reader to trust the servant's sincerity. The servant's tactics, however, are questionable; he proposes a simplistic test. He tells God that the woman from whose jar he requests a drink, the woman who obliges not only him, but who offers to water his camels, will be the designated bride. Although the test stems from the servant's initiative, and not from God's, he presumes it is acceptable. While it is true that the resolution of this test represents God's will rather than a simple coincidence, significantly, God does not respond to it. Thus, without being judgmental, the narrator provides details that cause the reader to question the appropriateness of the servant's plan and to appreciate God's providence.

The narrator has skillfully set the background for the next scene. All the women of the *city* of Nahor go to the well at evening. This is related twice, first in the narrator's words (24:10, 11), and secondly by the servant (24:13). The reader wonders, to how many of these women must the servant address his request before he finds a daughter of the *person* Nahor?[9] By the nature of the test he has devised, the servant has opened up countless possibilities.[10] The following information, related to the reader by the narrator, is not yet revealed to the servant.

> Before he had done speaking, behold, Rebekah, who was born to Bethuel the son of Milcah, the wife of Nahor, Abraham's brother, came out—and her water jar upon her shoulder. The maiden was very beautiful to look at, a virgin, and no man had known her (24:15-16).

It is clear that Rebekah's family origins are consonant with the information provided by the genealogy as well as by Abraham's instructions to the servant. The reader has two reasons to appreciate her appropriate status for Isaac. Her beauty captures the servant's attention; moreover, she is not married to another and is a virgin. The information that she has the water jug upon her shoulder is not a random detail, but rather prepares her to be addressed by the servant in the way that he told God he would raise the question—by referring to her water jar when requesting a drink. The reader is led to wonder, will the servant address her as he said he would? What will be her answer?

Although the servant does not ask Rebekah for water with the exact words that he told God he would use, the meaning remains intact (24:17; cf. 24:14); this paraphrase does not indicate any substantive change. Rebekah's response sets the context for an evaluation of her character. She responds solicitously, "Drink, my lord," and the narrator adds that she hastened to attend to the servant's needs, for "She hurried to let down her jar upon her hand, and gave him a drink" (24:18). The narrator uses "she hurried" (*těmahēr*) twice (24:18, 20) and "she ran" (*tārāṣ*, 24:30) to emphasize the deliberate action she took. The suspense of the account builds, however, as the narrator slows the pace and relates that only when she had finished giving him a drink does she mention the camels. Thus, the generosity of this woman is stressed. Her offer is not perfunctory; she not only promises to water the camels, but to do so until they are totally satisfied. From details presented earlier, the narrator underscores the difficulty of the task: there are ten camels she must water and she has only one water jug.[11]

As the next scene begins, it is not clear if Rebekah's response to the servant is enough for him to be certain of her family lineage. Although the generous response of the woman seems to fulfill the servant's quali-fication, the servant still does not know her lineage and status. The de-scription of the activity at this scene presents ambiguities. The most important clue is the comment by the narrator, "And the man wondered confusedly in silence *(mištā'ēh lāh maḥărîš)* to know whether YHWH grant-ed success on his journey or not" (24:21). The phrase "wondered con-fusedly" comes from the root *š'h* ("make a crash"), thus connoting confusion and astonishment.[12] The word for "in silence" points to someone who keeps silent even though he or she is angry, hurt, or confused. The word does not denote the kind of silence that comes from calm or peace-fulness.[13] The servant himself does not yet appear confident, nor does the narrator comment that the servant was assured. The narrator thereby con-tinues to augment the servant's uncertainty concerning her identity.[14]

Because of what he says and does, the servant unwittingly puts himself in difficult circumstances. He appears too hasty in his response to the initial meeting of Rebekah. Before he is certain of Rebekah's marital status or family origins, and before he knows that she is willing to go to Canaan (or her family will allow her to leave), he prematurely offers her the gifts from Abraham.[15] The haste of his actions is reflected by the difficult Hebrew that may be translated, "The man took a gold ring weighing half a shekel and two bracelets upon her arms weighing ten shekels" (24:22).[16] In the first phrase one would expect that the placement of the ring would be specified, in the second phrase one would expect that a verb of motion be used to indicate how the bracelets came upon her arms.[17] Although the wording of this phrase is difficult, the reference to the "two bracelets upon her arms" shows that she did receive the gifts. It is only with Rebekah's response to the servant's question, however, that he knows with certainty that she is of the same lineage as Abraham. She states, "I am the daughter of Bethuel, the son of Milcah, whom she bore unto Nahor" (24:24). Indeed, it is only after her revelation that the servant can say without doubt that God has led him to Abraham's relatives and can thank and worship God (24:26).[18] This use of dialogue and the commentary by the narrator show that the servant was not certain of the woman's identity when he gave her the gifts. Furthermore, the reader finds that the servant himself recognizes the potential error when he retells the account of his meeting to Laban (24:34-59).

By introducing such ambiguities, the narrator not only tells an engaging story, but also emphasizes God's protective care in providing the proper wife for Isaac. In spite of the servant's lack of precision in following Abraham's commands, the first episode of his encounter with Rebekah raises the reader's hopes that the servant has found the proper wife for Isaac.

Although the servant and the readers must wait for Rebekah's consent, it is already apparent that she is a woman who takes initiative. When the servant asks her if he might lodge at her home, she responds in the affirmative and does not tell him that she must first inquire with the family.[19] Moreover, we sense the seriousness with which she follows up on this request, for the narrator relates that Rebekah "ran and told her mother's household about these conversations" (24:28). Once again, *tārās* is used, recalling Rebekah's promptness in assisting the servant at the well.[20]

The focus of the account now turns to the response of Rebekah's family.[21] In spite of the positive introduction to Rebekah, the tension of the narrative continues because the introduction to her family raises the reader's suspicions. The narrator relates that the first thing her brother Laban reacts to is "the ring, and the bracelets upon his sister's arms" (24:30). The narrator withholds a full exposure of Laban's cunning character. Laban offers to care for the servant and his animals. Does he do this out of genuine concern, or because he sees that the servant must have a wealthy master? It is not until Laban appears again with the next generation, namely, with Jacob, Rachel, and Leah, that it becomes clear that he is untrustworthy and selfish.

Once the servant turns his attention to Rebekah's family, instead of to Rebekah herself, the narrator shows that he must await their response as well as hers. The long account wherein the servant relates his conversation with Rebekah as well as the one with Abraham should not be seen as primitive style or idle repetition. The narrator employs this technique to slow the pace of the account.[22] With Rebekah no longer at the center, the reader must wait and wonder about the outcome.

In noting exactly what the servant says to Laban in his recapitulation of the events, the reader discovers another use of the narrative technique that employs repetition of dialogue. A careful examination reveals that the servant changes some important details when retelling these accounts. He tells Laban incorrectly that Abraham had told him, "When you come to my family, and if they will not give her up to you, then you will be free from my oath" (24:41). However, Abraham had actually instructed him that he would be free from the oath "if the woman is not willing to come with you" (24:8). Even if it is assumed that it was customary to ask the family for permission, the servant misunderstands or misrepresents Abraham's point. Moreover, as will eventually be seen, Rebekah is the one who makes the decision to leave. In addition, as stated previously, the servant misrepresents what occurred earlier at the well when he first met Rebekah. At this point, perhaps recognizing his impetuousness in giving her the gifts before he knew of her family origins, the servant tells Laban that he inquired about her origins *before* he presented her with the jewelry.[23] The tone of his entire monologue stresses the servant's loyalty, service, and his trust in God even more than if he had related the account accurately. By conveniently rearranging events, the servant puts himself in good stead to receive a favorable reply from the family. His words reveal that he can exaggerate and err.[24] The reader obtains a greater appreciation of God's providence in guiding the servant to Rebekah when it is shown that the servant is careless on some crucial issues.

The family's initial response to the servant's request is given and it is a favorable one (24:50-51). Both Laban, Rebekah's brother, and Bethuel, Rebekah's father, answer for the family. Some interpreters have suggested that Bethuel's presence is secondary to the original account because he appears only at this later development and because Laban offered the servant hospitality; furthermore, the father does not speak again. Perhaps his appearance at this point is a result of the account's original multiple strands of tradition. By including the response of the father (24:50), the narrator lends impact to the decree.

The servant carelessly presumes that his task is over. He seems to forget the exact command that Abraham gave him because Rebekah herself has not yet given her consent to leave. Once again the servant showers gifts upon Rebekah as well as upon her brother and mother. In an arresting development, the next morning the brother and mother say that Rebekah should remain literally, "a few days, or ten" *(yāmîm ʾô ʿāśôr, 24:55).*[25] This idiomatic expression has the meaning, "several days." The servant immediately becomes uncomfortable, as does the reader, because the time specified is vague and potentially lengthy. The reader still awaits Rebekah's response. After the servant's insistence, the family finally asks Rebekah the long-awaited question: "Are you going with this man?" (24:58). Only at this point in the lengthy narrative is her answer given in her own words, "And she said, I will go" (24:58).[26] While it might be argued that Rebekah's decision is not crucial because the family had already agreed to her departure, it is clear that the narrator does not allow the reader to rest until this point. Until now, many contingencies could have kept Rebekah from leaving with the servant, and she was free to remain.[27] Recalling the servant's oath to Abraham and the one contingency that Abraham allowed that frame this account, it is apparent that Rebekah's answer is the climax of this narrative.

Keeping in mind that the first matriarch is dead, the reader now looks at Rebekah as the next mother of Israel. By skillfully referring to her nurse, maids, and the blessing that her family gives to her, her potential as mother is reflected. Obviously she will need the nurse and maids when she has her own children.[28] Her family blesses her in a manner that recalls the blessing given to Abraham (24:60). Rebekah will indeed continue to provide descendants.

It is only in the final scene that the narrator assures the reader that Rebekah has made the journey safely. The perspective is now that of Isaac. The camels, which Rebekah once watered, are now the ones that carry Isaac's bride. Rebekah covers herself with a veil when the servant tells her that Isaac approaches, perhaps indicating her status as a bride. Isaac raises no objections and immediately accepts her. Indeed, Isaac's immediate response is to take Rebekah into his tent to consummate their relationship. Finally, the reader is reminded of the connection between the matriarchs and of the heightened necessity of a wife for Isaac, especially after the death of Sarah, by the final phrase of this section: "So Isaac was comforted after his mother" (24:67).[29] Rebekah takes over Sarah's role. The narrator does not include any verbal response of Rebekah, nor is there any reflection on her reaction. Nonetheless, the narrator has shown that the woman who had undertaken a lengthy journey with a servant of questionable reliability continues on a path that fulfills her promise to travel to the foreign land and marry the unknown son of the servant's master. The reader's first impression is that Rebekah is a woman of courage.

Rebekah's Pregnancy (Gen. 25:19-26)

Unlike the long account that stressed the inability of Sarah to conceive, or the narratives that treat Rachel's long-term barrenness, the story of Rebekah's infertility is brief.[30] It is important to note that if a couple were unable to conceive, the assumption in ancient Israel was that the problem invariably was with the woman. With a rapid pace the narrator speaks of her inability to conceive, Isaac's prayer on her behalf, and her conception: "And Isaac entreated YHWH on behalf of his wife, because she was barren; and YHWH granted his prayer, and Rebekah his wife became pregnant" (25:21).

The narrator quickly shifts the focus from the reality of conception itself to the type of pregnancy that Rebekah endures. Unlike the other matriarchs, Rebekah's suffering comes from the pregnancy. The Hebrew text is obscure; it may be translated: "If it is thus, why is it that . . ." (25:22).[31] Translators have attempted to explain this statement, but ultimately it proves to be elusive. The excessively speculative suggestions that Rebekah considered suicide should be avoided.[32] It is, however, true that Rebekah was distraught enough "to inquire of YHWH" (25:22). God's revelation to her is crucial for understanding the remainder of the Rebekah narrative. Rebekah's relationships with Isaac and Esau must be understood in light of this oracle. God directly informs her of the plan that two nations will come forth from her sons.[33] It is noteworthy that Rebekah alone receives word of God's plans for her sons. Isaac is not informed of this important information; no reason is given. She understands at the beginning of her pregnancy that the younger son is destined to carry on the covenantal promise. Although the narrator does not explicitly state why Rebekah prefers Jacob to Esau (25:28), the use of epithets is most significant. Jacob is described as "a man of integrity (*ʾîš tām*), dwelling in tents" in contrast to his brother Esau, "a knowledgeable hunter, a man of the field" (25:27).[34] Besides this characteristic of temperament, which apparently endeared Jacob to Rebekah, the narrator's placement of the discussion of her feelings for her son in the context of the oracle gives rise to the possibility that God's destiny for her sons has an impact on Rebekah's feelings for them.[35] The troubled relationship between the brothers is presented immediately. Their birth is characterized by strife, and even in their youth, "Esau held his firstborn privilege in contempt" (25:34).[36] However, before the climax of this problem is related, the account of the strife between Jacob and Esau is interrupted. The narrator interjects the account of the potential struggle of Isaac and Rebekah with Abimelech, the king of Gerar.

Rebekah in Danger (Gen. 26:1-16)

A familiar theme appears. The account of a famine, which prompted Abraham to travel and to deceive a local ruler by stating that his wife was his sister, has occurred twice before in the accounts concerning Abraham and Sarah (chapters 12 and 20).[37] This text also deals with a threat to the covenantal promise. Verses 1–6 emphasize God's protection of Isaac and his promise of land and descendants in the face of the threatening famine.[38]

Rebekah, not Isaac, captures the reader's sympathies in this account, although she does not speak. Her silence is an indication of her powerless status in this story. In fact, the impression of Rebekah given in this scene differs from that of the strong and independent woman we saw earlier—

a woman who would speak to a male stranger, make her will known to her family, and inquire of God.

Isaac dominates here, but the narrator presents his actions in a questionable manner. He allows his fears to overwhelm him. Rather than trusting in God's assurance, he endangers both Rebekah and himself. Indeed, Isaac appears to consider only his own welfare. He tells the men of Gerar that this companion is his sister, "lest the men of the place should slay me on account of Rebekah" (26:7). However, by the use of additional information in the account, the narrator emphasizes that Isaac had no need to fear the men. God had specifically warned Isaac not to go to *Egypt*—that was where the danger lay. While in Gerar, God told him to "dwell in this land, and I will be with you" (26:3). Indeed, God continues to assure Isaac that the faithfulness shown to Abraham will be shown to him, and that the same promise given to Abraham will also be given to him (26:2-4). God also reminds Isaac of Abraham's obedience to "all of YHWH's commandments" (26:5).

It is all the more arresting in this context, therefore, that Isaac is willing to place his wife in danger. Not only does he demonstrate poor judgment in placing Rebekah at risk, but Isaac appears foolish when he openly plays with or fondles Rebekah in such a way that Abimelech can readily discern that she is his wife (26:8). The text highlights this by the play on words between *yiṣḥāq* (Isaac) and *měṣaḥēq* (playing/fondling) because both words come from the Hebrew root *ṣḥq* (laugh). Isaac's fear, therefore, appears as a lack of trust in God.

In contrast to the negative portrayal of Isaac's actions, the narrator portrays Abimelech in a positive manner. Unlike Isaac, who placed his wife in danger, Abimelech understands the gravity of his crime (26:10). The needlessness of Isaac's fear is evident when the reader learns that Abimelech continues to protect Isaac and Rebekah even after he discovers the deception. Instead of punishing Isaac, he instructs his people to refrain from harming the couple and threatens death to any who disobey. God's faithfulness to Isaac is reinforced by the fact that Isaac is not only protected from his own foolishness, but is also bountifully blessed after this incident.[39] When the account is completed, the reader is relieved to learn that Rebekah is unharmed and is moved to discover that, like Sarah, she was almost abused because of her husband's fear. The narrator has allowed Rebekah to capture the reader's sympathies before it is shown that she uses deception to obtain the blessing from Isaac. Moreover, because Isaac has already deceived Abimelech, his own deception by Rebekah comes as less of a surprise.

Reflection on the Marriages of Esau
(Gen. 26:34-35)

Following the description of Isaac and Rebekah's stay at Gerar, there is a brief reference to Esau and his marriages to foreign women. The brevity of this account, however, belies its importance. Esau marries two Hittite women "and they were a bitterness of spirit for Isaac and Rebekah" (26:34). Although we cannot be certain of the original context in which this information was used, it is strategically placed in its current position. When the reader last saw Esau, he blithely spurned his birthright. At this next encounter, he disregards his heritage and marries foreigners on two occasions. There is no doubt of the consequences: both parents are dismayed. The polemic against foreign marriages is not against foreigners per se, but rather reflects the concern that Israelites not adopt foreign religious practices and customs that threaten their own. Because Esau is of the second generation, any marriage outside of Abraham's family would seriously threaten the integrity of the nascent group.

The reader knows that Esau's behavior is not entirely unexpected, given the content of the birth announcement as well as the previously related information concerning his behavior with his younger brother. This new development only confirms what was revealed about Esau earlier. Clearly, the narrator's sympathies are not with Esau at this point.

Rebekah's Role in Obtaining the Blessing
for Jacob (Gen. 27:1-17)

Within the larger section of the deception of Isaac (27:1-40) is found a description of Rebekah's role in obtaining the blessing for Jacob (27:1-17). Usually, her role is assessed pejoratively by modern commentators. One commentator has suggested that Rebekah finds the system of primogeniture unfair and is rising up against the exclusive privilege of the eldest son, but by fighting for the rights of one son she actually is harming the other unfairly.[40] Others state that Rebekah's behavior demonstrates tension between her and Isaac, or shows that she was unkind or cruel. Finally, some suggest that we are simply given no information to account for her actions.[41] It is true that the narrator does not elaborate on Rebekah's motivation directly. However, these speculations ignore a most important clue that does come from the narrative. In its current placement in the sequence of information given about Rebekah, Isaac, Jacob, and Esau, this scene follows the oracle of the twins' birth, Esau's cavalier selling of his birthright, and Esau's marriage to foreign women. Isaac has not been told God's plan for the sons; that has been the privilege of Rebekah. Therefore, it is not surprising that Rebekah ensures that the son singled out by God receives the proper blessing from Isaac.[42] The narrator gives information to understand Rebekah's motivation. She knows from the birth oracle that Jacob is God's chosen. In addition, Esau's sale of his birthright confirms that he is not entitled to the first blessing. One cannot impugn that she is having strained marital relations with Isaac, that she is fighting a perceived injustice, or that the narrator has given no clues to understand her behavior. The narrator does not state why she chose this particular method of obtaining the birthright for Isaac, but she is only one of many persons who use deception; Jacob and Laban are prime examples.

Rebekah's feelings toward her two sons are particularly recounted by the narrator's address of Esau and Jacob in the beginning of this account: "Now Rebekah was listening when Isaac spoke to Esau *his son* (*běnô*). So when Esau went to the field to hunt for game and bring it, Rebekah said to Jacob *her son* (*běnâ*) . . ." (27:5-6). It is clear that Rebekah favors Jacob. Indeed, throughout the account, Esau is referred to as Rebekah's son only by the narrator (27:15, 42). Rebekah consistently calls Jacob "my son," and refers to Esau as Jacob's brother. In contrast, Isaac refers to Esau as "my son" and never refers to Jacob as "son," except when he thinks Jacob is Esau. The distinguishing use of "son" can be seen again in the blessing from Isaac. When Isaac states, "The smell of my son is as the smell of a field that YHWH has blessed" (27:27), he supposes he is addressing Esau. Similarly, when he states, "Be lord over your brothers, and may your mother's sons bow down to you" (27:29 RSV), he uses "mother's sons" to refer to Jacob.

Like Sarah, who listened at the tent door and heard the revelation of the birth of the child who would fulfill God's promise,[43] Rebekah hears important information about Isaac's plans to bless Esau. Once she begins to speak, her manner is deliberate and authoritative. In order to impress Jacob with the importance of the task, she hides no details. She tells Jacob what Isaac has told Esau. She accurately paraphrases Isaac's words, but when she refers specifically to the blessing that Isaac will give, she adds that it will occur "before YHWH" (27:7), thus emphasizing the significance of the blessing. Her authoritative posture is further stressed when she tells her son, "Hearken to my voice as I command you" (27:8). The reader already knows that any objection on Jacob's part will be countered by his mother.

After her warning, she explains the complete plan in detail. The narrator accelerates the pace of her commands, thus impressing their urgency. Although Isaac had requested unspecified game from Esau, Rebekah tells Jacob to bring her two kids. Besides obtaining these before Esau returns, the kids' skins are used to disguise the smooth texture of Jacob's skin. Rebekah's role in the plan is as significant as Jacob's. A series of imperatives punctuates her speech: "*Hearken to* my voice," "*go now* to the flock," "*fetch me* two good kids of the goats from there" (27:8-9). After Jacob obtains the kids, Rebekah prepares them. When Jacob objects that he will be detected because he is "a smooth man" whereas Esau is "hairy," he is immediately countered by his mother.[44] When Jacob protests, Rebekah's answer allows for no retort: "Upon me be your curse, my son" (27:13). In addition, she repeats to Jacob, "Hearken to my voice," and gives two additional commands in haste: "Now go—fetch for me!" (27:13). Yet, Rebekah does not simply wait, but rather acts to ensure that the plan will succeed. She obtains Esau's clothing for Jacob and prepares the skins of the kids to be placed on Jacob's hands and neck (27:15-17). Rebekah's plan succeeds; although Isaac is suspicious, Jacob does receive his father's blessing. When the ruse is discovered, neither Jacob nor Rebekah is cursed.

In a recent study, Esther Fuchs argues that although Rebekah must use deception to accomplish her goals because of her powerlessness in a patriarchal culture, the narrator does not make this explicit, thereby perpetuating an androcentric reading of the text that stereotypes women as untrustworthy. She further suggests that Isaac's helpless condition makes Rebekah appear particularly unkind.[45] However, the narrative details of Isaac's blindness and infirmity are used to show how Rebekah's plan could possibly succeed. Deception is typically used by powerless characters in the Bible—it is not a trait limited to women. This account, so important for an understanding of the role of Rebekah and her characterization in the Genesis narrative, shows that Rebekah acted decisively to ensure that Isaac's blessing is awarded to the son designated by God to carry on the promise. She does not act unfairly to Esau nor to Isaac, but skillfully completes the task initiated by God. Rebekah thus plays a crucial role in the ancestral narratives by ensuring the continuation of the promise for future generations.

Rebekah's Protection of Jacob
(Gen. 27:41—28:5)

Source-critical analysis, which identifies units of narratives that ultimately go back to different authors, would stress the distinct origins of the accounts in 27:41-45 and 27:46—28:9. The first scene indicates that Jacob left for Haran because of Rebekah's fear that Esau would kill him. The second scene emphasizes that Jacob left because of Isaac's admonitions. The first episode is now examined.

As the scene of Isaac's blessing of Jacob ends, once more Rebekah must protect Jacob. This time something greater is at stake than obtaining the blessing; now Jacob's life is in danger because Esau plans to kill him. Once again, Rebekah discovers the plan. She repeats the command she gave Jacob that enabled him to receive Isaac's blessing: "Hearken to my voice," followed by the imperatives, "Now get up, flee" (27:43). In the face of Jacob's danger from his brother, Rebekah relies on her own brother to protect Jacob. Her own role in guaranteeing Jacob's safety continues; she tells him that she will send for him when it is safe to return.

In the second episode Rebekah complains to Isaac that she does not want Jacob to marry Hittite women, as did Esau, and therefore, that Jacob should go to the city of her origins for a wife. She gives no indication to him that Esau plans to kill Jacob. Whatever the original sources of these episodes, by the placing of this account in sequence with the one found in 27:41-45, it is clear that the narrator intended that they be read as two scenes of one event. Rebekah has again obtained a blessing for Jacob. By telling Isaac that Jacob must go to her family for a wife, and not in order to escape Esau's wrath, Rebekah not only avoids potential conflict with Isaac over the earlier deception, but also prompts Isaac to give Jacob an additional blessing. Most importantly Isaac says to Jacob, "May he [God Almighty] give the blessing of Abraham to you and to your descendants with you, that you may take possession of the land of your sojournings which God gave to Abraham!" (28:4 RSV). Without a doubt, Jacob is now the inheritor of God's promises to Abraham and Isaac.

Conclusions

After her role in obtaining the blessing is completed, the remainder of Rebekah's life is not considered. The only other additional information given concerns Rebekah's death: Jacob later relates that she and Isaac are buried in the cave of Machpelah (49:31). It is not surprising that information about her life ends after the blessing for Jacob has been obtained. She has made the continuation of Abraham and Sarah's line possible, and has ensured that God's blessing will be continued through the son that God chose.

From the nature of her role, one might conclude that the narrator's use of Rebekah is quite limited. However, the characterization of Rebekah yields a deeper understanding of her significance. Rebekah was first shown as a beautiful woman who was kind and generous. If the only additional glimpse of her were in the scene where Isaac encounters the Gerarites and Abimelech, the reader might think of her as submissive. However, the totality of the presentation of Rebekah is as complex as are human beings. She is forthright in expressing her desires and feelings. She gives a resounding affirmation of her willingness to risk going to Canaan with the servant to meet a stranger. She expresses her pain and anxiety over her difficult pregnancy and openly laments Esau's marriages to foreign women. She inquires of God without hesitation, and God speaks to her. She risks her husband's curse in obtaining the blessing for Jacob and continues to protect him when he is threatened by Esau. All of these actions are given without a polemical context, and the narrator does nothing to indicate that these were unusual activities for a woman to take. Although the ancestors of Israel are idealized characters, their specific characterizations are often those with which people can readily identify.

A current approach among some biblical commentators in assessing the role of Rebekah is to compare her to Isaac. For example, two authors have argued that she should be seen to be more important than Isaac because she, and not Isaac, determines that the promise to Abraham is fulfilled.[46] Although past lack of interest in Rebekah makes such revisionary attempts understandable, this is not a fair way to study either Rebekah or Isaac. The portrayal of each ancestor must be examined carefully to understand their full significance for the narrator who wove various strands of tradition into the finished narrative. The portrayal of Rebekah shows that the community recognized her importance. The presentation of Rebekah shows that women in Israel were viewed as persons who could make crucial decisions about their futures, whose prayers were acknowledged, who might know better than men what God designed, and who could appropriately take the steps necessary to support God's plans for the community.

6

Rachel and Leah

Rival Daughters
of a Manipulative Father

The stories of Rachel and Leah are recorded because, like Sarah and Rebekah, these women continue the generations of nascent Israel. Rachel and Leah, who are sisters, become the wives of the patriarch Jacob. Along with their maids Bilhah and Zilpah, they give birth to thirteen children—twelve sons and a daughter. The twelve sons become the eponymous ancestors of the twelve tribes of Israel and Leah's daughter Dinah becomes a pawn in the disastrous struggle between her brothers and the Shechemites.[1] The narratives of Rachel and Leah, preserved to propel the history of their people forward, also probe the difficulties of family relationships, the consequences of deception, and the special suffering of women due to their ability to have children.

Introduction to Rachel (Gen. 29:1-12)

Rachel is introduced in the narrative after Jacob approaches the vicinity of Haran, his ancestral land, to search for a wife. Paralleling Abraham's servant who, upon his arrival in Haran, discovered Rebekah as a bride for Isaac, Jacob, too, finds his future bride at the well. By creating the familiar scene, the narrator at first raises our expectations that Jacob will be successful in finding a bride. Indeed, Jacob quickly encounters shepherds who come from Haran and know Laban. Laban, the brother of Rebekah, was featured in the earlier account of the servant's search for Isaac's bride; he will now hold the key to Jacob's success in finding a wife.

The narrator withholds an immediate introduction to Laban in order to prolong the drama. Jacob learns from the shepherds that Laban is well. However, before he meets him, the shepherds point out to Jacob that Laban's daughter, Rachel, approaches.[2] This pastoral scene suggests fertility: Rachel, whose name means "ewe," is accompanied by her sheep. Although the maternal imagery is obvious, it is ironic that Rachel will struggle for many years before she will ever have children. The abundance of sheep at the scene is also proleptic of Jacob's future success as a shepherd and breeder of sheep in spite of the unfair circumstances that Laban creates.

Jacob's first attempt to be alone with Rachel fails. He encourages the other shepherds to go and pasture their sheep as Rachel approaches. They respond, however, that they must wait for all the shepherds to arrive in order to roll the stone away from the well. This detail foreshadows the upcoming seven years of waiting that Jacob must endure for Rachel. At the same time the stone at the well gives Jacob an opportunity to impress Rachel because, upon her arrival, he single-handedly removes it and waters her sheep. His strength and care for the sheep also set the stage for the long years of work he will labor for Laban's flocks.[3]

The narrator conveys the moving quality of the meeting of Jacob and Rachel by revealing their own perspectives. Jacob's response is emotional: "Then Jacob kissed Rachel, and lifted up his voice and wept" (29:11). Rachel's actions also convey her powerful emotions. When Jacob explains his origins, she immediately "ran and told her father" (29:12). However, the narrator's description of Rachel remains incomplete. It is apparent that she is a shepherd, but the narrator records neither direct speech nor a personal description. Instead the focus quickly turns to her father Laban, who manipulates both his daughters' lives and forces them into a situation that will cause them much suffering.

Laban's Manipulation of Rachel and Leah
(Gen. 29:13-30)

Just as Laban ran to meet Abraham's servant upon his arrival, so too does he approach Jacob with haste. This parallel description prompts the reader to consider whether Laban will respond as greedily to the prospects of having a daughter married as he did when his sister Rebekah was to be married to Isaac. Initially, the narrator withholds any negative description of Laban's actions toward Jacob or his daughters. The narrator simply writes that Laban welcomed Jacob warmly.

A month after Jacob's arrival, however, Laban says to Jacob, "Should you serve me gratuitously?"—literally, "Should you serve me out of favor?" (29:15). The narrator's choice of the phrase "out of favor" (*hinnām*) also means "for no purpose" or "in vain."[4] This negative connotation is appropriate because Jacob will soon be cheated by Laban. Although Laban at first appears generous by insisting that Jacob determine his wages, Laban's hurtful deception soon will become apparent. Jacob's service will in fact approximate working "in vain." Before Jacob responds, however, the narrator discloses that Laban has more than one daughter. Rachel, the first daughter encountered in the narrative, is not the eldest. Laban later uses this fact as an excuse for his deception of Jacob. The narrator's description of the sisters is terse but nonetheless prompts speculation. The narrator writes, "Leah's eyes were weak, but Rachel was beautiful in form and beautiful to look at" (29:17).[5] The narrator withholds information on the role Leah will play in Laban's plan. Indeed, the narrator does not record any reaction to Leah on Jacob's part. Instead, immediately after the narrator gives the physical description of the sisters, Jacob's indisputable attachment to Rachel is revealed. The narrator states that he loved her. Perhaps to modern sensibilities, Jacob's feelings appear to be based more on physical attraction than on genuine love, but the narrator does not make this distinction.

This juxtaposition of the sisters foreshadows the interconnectedness that will be forced upon them by their father's plot to trick Jacob into marrying both of them. It will not be the only time they are compared, and the irony soon will unfold. Although Rachel is beautiful, it is Leah who is fertile. Rachel's value to Jacob as a beautiful wife is apparent, whereas Leah's ability to bear children is hidden.

It is within this context that Jacob answers Laban's question about appropriate wages. He states that he will work for Laban for seven years in order to marry Rachel.[6] Jacob specifically identifies Rachel by name and refers plainly to her position in the family as "the younger." Thus, the narrator assures the reader that Jacob knows of the elder daughter Leah. Laban responds to Jacob cryptically. "It is better that I give her to you," he states, "than that I give her to another man. Stay with me" (29:19). Laban does not confirm that *seven* years are acceptable to him—indeed, his statement "stay with me" implies an indefinite period of time.

The narrator acknowledges that Jacob's seven years is a lengthy term of service and concomitantly stresses Jacob's love for Rachel by observing that seven years "seemed to him but a few days because of the love he had for her" (29:20 RSV).[7] This direct information from the narrator heightens the drama of the future revelation that Jacob is at first denied his beloved.

Strikingly, *Jacob* must remind Laban that his time of service is completed and that it is now his right to marry Rachel. After stating that the bargain must be completed, the narrator appropriately withholds Laban's response, preparing the reader for the upcoming deception. The narrator proceeds simply by indicating that preparations for the feast were made. Immediately after this brief description, the narrator reveals that Laban gives Leah to Jacob instead of Rachel, and that Jacob unknowingly consummates the marriage with Leah. Apparently, Laban presumes that Leah will be fertile and gives Zilpah to Leah as a servant—one who could be used as a nursemaid. This information is strategically placed after the information about Jacob's sexual union with Leah because Zilpah will become one of Jacob's concubines. Jacob's discovery that he has married Leah is powerfully disclosed by the succinct phrase: "and it was morning, and behold, it was Leah!" (29:25). It is appropriate that in referring to their sexual union, the narrator uses the expression "he went into her" (29:23 RSV) instead of the more common "he knew her," because Jacob did not even recognize his bride and certainly did not know her with any emotional intimacy.[8]

Jacob's shock and disbelief at Laban's deception are indicated by his quick succession of questions that do not allow for Laban's response. When Laban does speak, he does not answer Jacob's questions. Rather, he offers a pathetic excuse, saying that it is not customary that the younger daughter be married before the firstborn (29:26). The use of the term "firstborn" *(habběkîrâ)* by Laban (instead of "the elder" as used by the narrator above) recalls the earlier narrative where Jacob had lied to his father Isaac and said that he was "Esau, your firstborn" (*ʿēśāw běkōrekā*, 27:19). The term *bkr*, used in reference to both Leah and Esau, emphasizes the privilege that comes with the position of being born first.[9] It is also appropriate that instead of referring to Jacob's beloved Rachel by name, Laban condescendingly, or perhaps even contemptuously, refers to her as "this (one)" (29:27). The reader knows, of course, that Laban had remained silent about "the custom" when Jacob first asked to marry Rachel, and thus his reasoning does not appear sincere. Furthermore, Laban offers harsh terms to Jacob to ameliorate the consequences of the deception; he offers Rachel to Jacob as a wife in return for an additional seven years of labor. Surprisingly, Jacob agrees to these terms. Where Laban appears selfish, Jacob appears resigned, and he is desperate for Rachel. Their characterizations are also reflective of their status. Laban is the owner of great flocks, whereas Jacob is the young sojourner without means. After completing one week of marital relations and celebration with Leah, Jacob marries Rachel. Recalling Laban's present of a maid to Leah, Laban also gives a maid, Bilhah, to Rachel. However, in this instance the presence of the maid portends the necessity of a concubine in order for Rachel to have children.

The disparity in Jacob's feelings for the sisters is central: "He loved Rachel more than Leah" (29:30 RSV). The reader must wonder what the consequences of this preference will be for all four participants: Laban, who orchestrated the situation; Jacob, who loved Rachel from the moment he saw her; and the sisters, Leah and Rachel, who are forced to live their lives inextricably bound together through no desire or plan of their own.

The narrator has not yet provided any indication of the feelings that Leah and Rachel have for their father, their husband, or each other. While it is true that the narrative focuses more on what happens to Leah and Rachel rather than how they feel about each other, their father, and their husband, the narrator does convey their feelings by the content and placement of their comments and actions. At this point the narrative raises questions that become resolved only as it proceeds. What does Leah think about her father's use of her as a pawn to dupe Jacob? How does she feel toward her husband who so obviously loves her sister more? What is her response to her beautiful and beloved sister? What does Rachel think of her father who denied her the undivided love of Jacob? How does Rachel feel toward Leah who has a more privileged position as Jacob's first wife? Both Rachel and Leah are affected by the power of the patriarchal structures that dominate their lives. Will they always remain powerless in their relationships with their father and their husband?

God's Response to Leah (Gen. 29:31-35)

The narrator reports the unquestionable fact that Leah was hated by revealing this information from God's perspective. "When YHWH saw that Leah was hated," the narrator reports, God "opened her womb" (29:31). The word for "was hated" (śĕnûʾâ) may have connotations of sexual revulsion[10] and is an appropriate indicator of Jacob's feelings toward Leah. In fact, it later becomes clear that Jacob does not often sleep with Leah. Moreover, by placing this description of the hated Leah in the passive, the narrator allows the reader to speculate on the identity of those who hate Leah. They could include her father Laban, who, rather than providing her with a husband who might have her as the sole (and beloved) wife, chooses the convenience of having Jacob marry her—a man who is readily available and provides free labor for Laban's estate. Another possible source of hatred is Rachel. Later Deuteronomic legislation will prohibit the marriage of sisters to the same husband; the potential for conflict is obvious.[11] Indeed, the controversies between Rachel and Leah will soon appear.

The portrayal of God as the giver of fertility is dominant throughout the Hebrew Bible.[12] The narrator shows that Leah acknowledges God's role in the birth of her first child Reuben. The importance of having a child lies not only in the inchoate feelings of desire for parenthood, family, and posterity; it is also the only way for a woman to achieve status in her own family and community. This situation is reflected in the very word used to describe a woman who is infertile. One Hebrew word usually translated "barren" or "childless" (ʿarîrî) comes from the root meaning "strip," with connotations of destitution.[13] Another word meaning "barren" or "childless" (ʿāqār) comes from the root meaning "pluck" or "root up."[14] When Sarah finally has a child, she exclaims that other women will "laugh for me" (21:6). Although the phrasing is ambiguous, it is clear that Sarah's esteem among other women (as well as among men) is related to giving birth to her son. When Jephthah's daughter is about to be sacrificed, she first mourns "her maidenhood" (Judg. 11:37) in the mountains with her women friends—an obvious reference to her impending death before marriage and children. Leah, the elder daughter of Laban, the primary wife of Jacob in terms of position, is treated as a secondary wife by the man who prefers Rachel. Surely her children enable her to feel superior to her barren sister.[15] Thus, after giving birth to her first three sons (Reuben, Simeon, and Levi), Leah thanks God, but hopes that Jacob will come to love her as he loves Rachel. The lack of information on Jacob's response prompts the reader to consider the intractability of Leah's plight. With the birth of her fourth son Judah, Leah no longer connects God's gift as a redress for her being hated nor as a means to achieve her husband's love. For the first time in the naming of her sons, Leah does not refer to her affliction nor to her lack of love when she names Judah. She simply says, "This time I will praise YHWH" (29:35).[16] Leah's desire to be loved, however, does not truly abate, for at the births of her additional sons she again will express her hopes.

Rachel's Plight (Gen. 30:1-8)

The suffering that accompanies Rachel's inability to conceive is augmented by her sister's ease at conceiving by their shared husband. "And she envied her sister," the narrator reports, stressing not only Leah's ability to have children but also the intensity of feeling that can arise among family members (30:1). The word used for "envied" (*qn'*) is later used to describe the feelings of Leah's sons, who conspire against their brother Joseph, Rachel's son, the favored child of Jacob.[17] The first words of Rachel are dramatic. "Give me sons," she demands of Jacob, "or I will die" (30:1).[18] The intensity of the language arouses the reader's sympathies for the distraught Rachel.[19] Even if it may be doubted that her suffering would cause her death, the fact that she states that her emotions feel like the experience of dying cannot be denied. Jacob's response, declaring that only God has the power to close her womb, also comes from the experience of frustration.[20] The narrator emphasizes that both are powerless to ensure fertility. Only God can alter the situation.[21]

Like the childless Hannah, who admits to being anxious and pained (1 Sam. 1:16 RSV), Rachel pours out her heart. But unlike Hannah who addresses God, Rachel turns to her unsympathetic husband. Jacob's angry response is tantamount to a retort: "Am I in the place of God who has withheld from you the fruit of your womb?" (30:2). Although Jacob's acknowledgment of God's gift of fertility is correct, the tone of his reply is unkind. Rachel's response is desperate. She tells Jacob to have sexual relations with her maid Bilhah so that she might have children through her. The reader is reminded of the earlier case of surrogate motherhood, Sarah and Hagar. Might this event prompt similar tragedy? Surprisingly, the cases could not be more different. Scant attention is given to Bilhah, who bears two sons. Rachel names the children and claims them as her own. From her perspective, her decisiveness in a difficult situation brings her children, although the narrator does not consider Bilhah's response.[22]

The significance of God's role in allowing these pregnancies as well as the struggle between Rachel and Leah is demonstrated by Rachel's choice of names for the sons born to Bilhah. With the birth of the first son, Rachel names him Dan to indicate that God has "judged" her favorably (30:6). She names the second son Naphtali to show that she has struggled with her sister and prevailed (30:7-8).[23] Note that the births of these sons do not truly take away Rachel's anguish. Only with the birth of her biological son can she say that God has removed her reproach (30:23).

Leah's Response (Gen. 30:9-13)

Although Leah already has five sons, she continues to measure her worth by her ability to have children. Thus, when she no longer can have children, she follows Rachel's lead and uses her maid Zilpah to have more. Zilpah gives birth to two sons, whom Leah names Gad, associated with "good fortune," and Asher, which she links with the phrase, "in my happiness women (*bānôt*) will pronounce me happy" (30:13). The word choice for women refers especially to young women of child-bearing age who will more greatly esteem her, thus reflecting their own desires.[24] It is significant that with the naming of her children in these instances, Leah refers neither to Jacob nor to her quest to have him love or respect her, nor does she refer to any contest with Rachel. She does recognize, however, that the births of these additional sons make her more esteemed among women.

The Contest for the Fertility Plant
(Gen. 30:14-24)

Until this point in the narrative, the jealousy and conflict that exist between Leah and Rachel have been conveyed by the names of their children and the narrator's direct comment that Rachel was jealous of Leah. Now, for the first time, the two sisters are engaged in dialogue with one another. The depth of their feeling is demonstrated in this emotional scene when they determine who will sleep with Jacob. Their desire for Jacob is prompted by their need for children (for Rachel) and for companionship (for Leah).[25]

After Leah's son discovers some mandrakes, a plant associated with fertility and considered to be an aphrodisiac, Rachel makes her request of Leah: "Please give me some of your son's mandrakes" (40:14). Unlike her cry to Jacob, Rachel speaks politely and reservedly to Leah. By identifying the mandrakes as belonging to Leah's son, instead of to Leah herself, Rachel's statement makes Leah's possession of them appear less definite. The narrator consistently has both Leah and Rachel refer to them as "the son's mandrakes" throughout the scene.[26] Leah's response belies the depth of her anger and exasperation. In a forceful statement she cries, "Was it a small matter that you took my husband? Must you even take my son's mandrakes?" (30:15). This statement indicates that as the second but more beloved wife, Rachel has usurped Leah's position of privilege as first wife and firstborn. It also indicates that at some point in the marriage Rachel has obtained sexual monopoly of Jacob. By revealing this fact in Leah's outburst to Rachel, the narrator leaves open the possibility that Leah was ignored by Jacob's choice rather than by Rachel's conspiracy. Rachel avoids answering this accusation and instead offers to pay Leah for the mandrakes by having Jacob sleep with her. It is ironic that the women whose lives were circumscribed by their scheming father and insensitive husband presently control Jacob's sexual activity. Leah approaches Jacob and insists that he must sleep with her because she has hired him.[27]

Although the women control Jacob's sexual activity, it is God who controls fertility. Despite the absence of the mandrakes, Leah becomes pregnant. Leah not only becomes pregnant with a son from this encounter but also has an additional son as well as a daughter.[28] The narrator implies that Jacob begins to have sexual relations with her more frequently. With the naming of her two additional sons, Leah first acknowledges God as the giver of fertility and secondly notes the prestige that the births of these sons give her. Although she had earlier despaired that Jacob would never love her, her deep longing is still reflected in the naming of her son Zebulun. "God bestowed a great gift upon me," she cries. "This time," she continues, "my husband will dwell with me" / "will honor me" *(yizbĕlēnî)*, because I gave him six sons" (30:20). The ambiguity of the word that may be translated as "will dwell with me" or "will honor me" is appropriate. Although it would be expected that Jacob would honor the woman who bore him six sons, it is not likely that he will dwell with Leah because he prefers Rachel.

Just as Leah's pregnancies are not contingent upon the discovery and use of the mandrakes, neither is Rachel's, even though she presses for them so strongly. The report of Leah's three pregnancies after the initial discovery of the mandrakes indicates that almost three years have passed before Rachel finally becomes pregnant. Rachel conceives, not because of any plan of her own, but because God "listened to her" and "opened her womb" (30:22).

Rachel acknowledges God's role and declares that God has taken away her "reproach" *(herpâ)*—a word connoting scorn, shame, and disgrace (30:23).[29] Rachel hopes that the birth of the first child indicates that she will remain fertile. Thus, by naming her first son Joseph, she articulates her hope that another will be born with God's graciousness. By the expression of this hope, the narrator prompts the reader to consider whether another birth will in fact transpire and emphasizes God's role in her conception.

The contest of Rachel and Leah for the mandrakes prepares the reader for the forthcoming fertility of both women—the birth of two more sons and a daughter to Leah and a son to the long-infertile Rachel. One modern commentator argues that this scene shows the willingness of both sisters to work together against the strictures of the patriarchal system that controlled their lives.[30] However, the narrator does not use any detailed description or language to indicate that there is any genuine cooperation between Leah and Rachel. Leah is distraught when Rachel asks for the mandrakes and responds with an angry retort. It is only when Rachel bribes her with an opportunity to sleep with Jacob that Leah relinquishes them. After this scene the following incidents that concern Rachel and Leah do not contain any hint of the continuing struggle. However, this improvement in the relationship between Rachel and Leah is not due to any breakthrough that occurred during the contest over the mandrakes. It happens because Rachel can finally be at peace after she bears a child and also because both sisters unite in order to thwart the treachery of their father—whose selfishness will threaten their own children.

The struggle between Rachel and Leah clearly arises from a context of patriarchal structures and expectations. The narrator presents a society that determines the value of women by the number of sons they bear. The narrator shows that these women are desperate to become pregnant and bear sons in order to have the esteem of both men and women. At the same time, however, Rachel and Leah are shown to find great personal satisfaction in the births of their children. Surely, a combination of reasons exists for their sense of fulfillment. In a society that esteems sons, they have brought honor to themselves.[31] Their names for the children often reveal their sense of joy. Moreover, as Reuben's care for his mother (by bringing her the mandrakes) demonstrates, they have the companionship and love of their children. In their society women have few options for individual fulfillment other than having children.[32] The Hebrew Bible never acknowledges that childlessness is an acceptable alternative for a meaningful life for women or for men.[33] "Be fruitful and multiply" (1:28) is the first command of God in the Book of Genesis,[34] and fertility is always associated with blessing throughout the Hebrew Bible. In a society where population growth was desirable and equated with political strength, and where infant mortality was high, neither men nor women believed that not wanting children was acceptable. The stories of the matriarchs reveal the patriarchal goal of having sons to add to a man's prestige and material well-being. However, they also present the prominent theological perspective that the God who calls Abraham out of Ur keeps the promise of descendants and is a powerful God of fertility.[35]

Jacob's Decision to Leave Laban
(Gen. 30:25-43)

The narrator suggests that Jacob considers his family complete after Rachel gives birth to Joseph because only at this point does he request to return to his own land. Ostensibly, his father-in-law agrees. The narrator arouses the reader's suspicions about Laban's agreement by the way in which Laban suggests that Jacob be paid for his work. Just as Laban earlier suggested that Jacob determine his own wages, so too does he tell Jacob to name his price. It comes as no surprise, therefore, when Laban once more attempts to cheat Jacob. After agreeing that Jacob can have all the distinctively colored animals from his flocks, Laban removes them. Jacob, however, remains the successful trickster and prompts the animals to produce a great number of the properly colored offspring by clever techniques of animal husbandry.

The Response of Leah and Rachel
(Gen. 31:1-21)

In order to examine the next scene in which Rachel and Leah are featured, it is appropriate to consider the narrative context. After Jacob outwits Laban and obtains much of his livestock, Laban's sons become jealous and accuse Jacob of stealing what is rightfully theirs. When Jacob learns that Laban is disgruntled as well, God intervenes and informs him to return to the land of Canaan. The narrator's explanation of Laban and his sons' anger with Jacob as well as God's promise to be with Jacob enables the reader to perceive the danger that lies ahead for Jacob.

Surprisingly, the narrator shifts the focus to Rachel and Leah. Unlike the earlier scenario when Jacob first desired to leave, he now asks his wives' permission to leave their father's home. Recognizing that a break with Laban and Laban's sons at this point would put an irrevocable breach between his own immediate family and that of his wives, Jacob solicits their agreement. The reader now knows that Rachel and Leah will either confirm or deny God's plans for Jacob; their decision is binding. Thus, the narrator shows that Jacob's appeal to them is detailed and definitive. In a lengthy speech, Jacob relates the history of Laban's injustice to him and God's revelation to him, thereby strengthening his plea that the family should leave (31:4-13).

Rachel and Leah, for the first time, speak in a united voice. The sisters who competed for Jacob's love and for status in society now recognize the injustice done to them by their father and answer Jacob with solidarity. It is appropriate that they disown their father in the formulaic words that are reminiscent of other important family ruptures in the Hebrew Bible: "Do we yet have a portion or inheritance in our father's house?"

(31:14).[36] They continue to defy their father with these arresting words: "We are regarded by him as foreigners because he has sold us and he even devoured our money" (31:15). The word chosen for "foreigners" (nāk-rîyyôt) has negative connotations. Solomon's idolatrous wives, for example, are referred to by this term as are the Babylonian women that Ezra and Nehemiah condemn as potential marriage partners for exiled Jewish men.[37] The word for "devour" (yōʾkal) implies ruthlessness of action. By this language, the narrator indicates how utterly estranged Rachel and Leah are from their father. They continue to express the rage that they feel toward him: "All the riches which God snatched away (hiṣṣîl) from our father are ours and our children's" (31:16).[38] The word choice for "snatch away" has the connotation of rescue in time of trouble, thereby emphasizing the unfairness of their father's treatment of them and their children. Rachel and Leah act with strength and independence. The father who had exploited his daughters by the problematic marriages he arranged for them continues to cheat them by denying payment to their households and to their children. By these details, the narrator shows that they rightfully feel betrayed.

By their decision to break with their father, Rachel and Leah legitimize Jacob's wishes and enable God's plans for Jacob to be actualized. The narrator shows that these woman play an important role in the continuation of Israel's nascent history. The importance of Rachel and Leah lies not only in their role as the bearers of Jacob's children and the means by which God fulfills the promise of descendants, but also as the decision makers who secure the future for their descendants in the land of the promise.[39]

The Family Departs (Gen. 31:17-23)

The narrator depicts a departure scene that reveals the riches that Jacob has accumulated and the finality of the break of the family from Laban. Jacob provides camels, a sign of wealth, for his sons and wives to ride upon during the journey to Canaan. The narrator hints at an important scene to come: Rachel steals her father's household gods. Although the narrator does not give a motive, the previous scene has set the context. Both Leah and Rachel are furious with their father. Rachel, like Jacob, tricks Laban out of something important to him.[40] The comparison is appropriately suggested by the narrator, since immediately after the information is given that Rachel stole the gods, the narrator reports that Jacob "outwitted Laban the Aramean" (31:20 RSV). Both Rachel and Jacob have tricked Laban, who is now identified as the outsider by the narrator's reference to him as the Aramean (31:20; see also 31:24).

The Threat to Rachel (Gen. 31:22-35)

Laban pursues Jacob, Leah, Rachel, and the children with tenacity, setting the stage for a worrisome encounter. However, the narrator addresses the reader's uncertainty by indicating that God appears to Laban in a dream and warns him not to harm Jacob. The narrator continues to build the suspense by a superb plot, however. When Laban reaches Jacob, he speaks to him in a hostile tone. Laban badgers Jacob with accusations that are asked with such haste that Jacob, at first, has no time to answer. Confronting Jacob, Laban claims that by sneaking away, he denied him a chance to send Jacob away with feasting and to wish his daughters and grandchildren well. Laban's previous actions make him appear insincere. The reader knows that when Jacob previously asked Laban's permission to leave, Laban made no such preparations. Moreover, Laban attempted to impoverish Jacob—making travel impossible.

The narrator delays Laban's declaration that God appeared to him. This encourages the reader to suppose that he might withhold this crucial information from Jacob and continue to badger him. However, after bragging that he is capable of harming him, Laban admits that God commanded him not to do so. After acknowledging the God of Jacob, in a supreme display of irony, Laban reveals his most crucial question—"Why did you steal my gods?" (31:30). The reader, knowing that Rachel has stolen them, wonders whether Laban's wrath might endanger Rachel. The suspense builds when Jacob, in his ignorance, declares that "whomever you find with your gods shall not live" (31:32). In earlier narratives, Abraham and Isaac knowingly put their wives in danger. This time Jacob does so through his own ignorance and frustration with Laban's accusations. The reader wonders what fate will befall Rachel.

The narrator continues to build the suspense. Laban searches the tents of Jacob, Leah, and the maids, respectively. The narrator permits the reader to know the location of the gods; Rachel put them on the camel saddle upon which she sits. Entering Rachel's tent, Laban "felt about" *(yĕmaššēš)* the tent (31:34). The reader must wonder—will he search the camel saddle?

The narrator shows that Rachel is indeed very clever. She tells her father that she cannot get up from the camel saddle because "the way of women is upon me" (31:35 RSV). The expression is an obvious reference to menstruation. The place upon which she sits would be considered unclean by the narrator's audience, and thus Laban would not be able to "feel about" the camel saddle. By the word choice for "feel about" (31:34, 37) the narrator recalls the earlier deception of Jacob, who worries that Isaac would "feel" him and know he was not Esau (27:12).[41] The reader is relieved to know that Laban, continuing the search, does not find the gods, and thus departs.[42]

Was Rachel indeed menstruating, or did she deceive her father? The narrator does not give any more information to judge the veracity of her words. But in either case, Rachel appears strong and is able to outwit her father, a trickster himself. Either Rachel took advantage of the fact that she was menstruating by sitting on the hidden gods, or she invented the tale in order to save her life. In the final analysis she is victorious over the father who used her and then ignored her. Earlier, along with Leah, she had disowned Laban. Now, she defeats him by using the only weapon available to her—her wits.[43] This is the only occasion in the accounts of the matriarchs where an ancestress in danger provides her own protection.[44]

One commentator has argued that the narrator presents Rachel negatively. Since the motivation for her theft of the gods is not specified, she appears as an idolator herself.[45] However, the context of this account shows that Rachel took the gods after her expression of bitter anger against Laban's treatment of her and her son. Rachel's anger is legitimized by the fact that Leah, who previously was in contention with Rachel, agrees with her sister during the condemnation. The theft of the gods is presented as another act of trickery in which Rachel succeeds against the man who deceived her and her family.[46] Moreover, Rachel's own reference to her ritual impurity implies that she shows little deference to the gods and treats them merely as objects of her father's property. It is difficult to contend that the narrator wants the reader to believe that Rachel valued the gods for their own sake if she would sit upon them in her genuine or feigned ritually impure state.[47] More important is the context of the continuing narrative. If there remains any doubt that Rachel values the household gods of her father, the reader soon discovers that all members of Jacob's household gave up their gods at his request (35:1-4). Although no one is explicitly mentioned, the narrator does not exclude Rachel. The narrator clearly conveys that the gods of Laban are weak. Laban cannot find them while Rachel sits upon them and seemingly mocks them. In the meantime, the God of Jacob triumphs. This God appears to Laban in a dream and dissolves his potent hostility. This God leads Jacob and his family into the land of the promise, accompanied by the many other visible signs of God's promise, including the children of Leah, Rachel, and their maids.

Jacob's Confrontation with Laban and Its Aftermath (Gen. 31:36-55)

Rachel's clever ruse also prompts Jacob to challenge Laban confidently for the first time. Forcefully, Jacob condemns Laban for being unfair to him. Laban is unable to acknowledge Jacob's perspective on the history of their relations because he insists that he still owns his daughters, their children, and the flocks. Nonetheless, he agrees to a pact with Jacob. Ironically, Laban insists that Jacob treat his daughters well and warns Jacob not to take any other women as wives. However, it was Laban who initially treated them poorly and created the situation where neither of them could be the only wife of one man. It was also he who gave Leah and Rachel the maids who later became wives or concubines of Jacob as well.[48]

Despite the disastrous relationship between Laban and his daughters, the final glimpse that the reader has of him hints of a partial reconciliation. The narrator states that Laban kisses and blesses his daughters and grandchildren before he departs. By withholding a description of Rachel and Leah's reaction to their father, the narrator allows the reader to speculate on their feelings and reaction, thus preserving ambiguity. This lessening of hostilities foreshadows the reconciliation between Jacob and Esau, the narrative that immediately follows.

Additional Glimpses of Leah and Rachel

Although Leah and Rachel do not figure prominently in the narrative of Jacob's journey to Canaan and his meeting with Esau, the narrator's references to the women in this account underscore their continuing importance.

Upon entry into the land, Jacob learns that Esau is preparing to meet him (32:1-8). The scene appears ominous; the brother whom Jacob had tricked and who wanted to kill Jacob appears with a large number of troops. The reader's attention is drawn to the wives and children of Jacob. Will they survive, and thus, will the people survive? Jacob's favoritism to Rachel appears again. In preparing his family to meet Esau, he places Rachel and her child in the most distant, hence the safest, position away from Esau and his troops. Leah, in turn, is favored over Zilpah and Bilhah, because she is in the middle position between the servants and Rachel.

Like all previous incidents in which the ancestresses of Israel were in danger and later rescued, here too Leah and Rachel are saved. Esau is willing to be reconciled with Jacob and no longer can be considered a threat.

Rachel's Death (Gen. 35:16-21)

It should not be surprising that the final narrative about the wives of Jacob concerns Rachel alone. Just as the narrative of the meeting of Rachel begins the introduction to both Rachel and Leah, Rachel's death ends the narrative development of these women. Leah's death is not mentioned in the Bible, but Rachel's features prominently because it is connected with the birth of her second son as well as the establishment of a memorial for her.

Earlier in her life, Rachel pleaded with her husband, "Give me sons or I will die" (30:1). However, it is actually in giving birth to her second child that she does in fact suffer and die.[49] Appropriately, Rachel names her son Benoni, meaning "son of my anguish" (35:18). After her death, Jacob renames the child Benjamin, meaning "son of the south" or "son of my right hand" (35:18). This name is appropriate since Rachel is presented as giving birth to Benjamin in the southern territory of the land of Canaan, the land that will become known as Judah. This renaming should not be seen as an example of Jacob's encroachment on Rachel's right to name her son but should be interpreted as a sign of hope.[50] Indeed, Jacob expresses his love for Rachel even in death. He sets up a monument to her, which continues, in popular tradition, to the narrator's present time (35:19-20).[51]

Conclusions

The narrator does not hide the fact that Leah and Rachel have difficult lives. Because of their father's scheme, they are forced into marriages filled with tension and disappointments. Rachel's story demonstrates the bitterness of childlessness in a world where women's worth was measured by the number of sons they bore. Leah's story, which shows the rejection by her husband for his prettier wife, underscores the suffering that women endure when their value is determined by physical beauty.

Despite their powerlessness in the face of their father's or husband's actions, the narrator does show that these women could act with independence and strength. Although Leah understandably waivers between resigning herself to the lack of Jacob's love and still hoping for it, she often shows courage by acknowledging God's gift of the many sons given to her and not relying on her husband's approval. Rachel takes the initiative to have children through her maid. Not satisfied, she pursues fertility through Leah's mandrakes. Although the narrator ultimately concludes that God determines fertility, the mandrakes incident shows that the women could determine when and with whom Jacob would have sexual relations. This is astonishing when it is recalled that previously it was their father who determined Jacob's sexual unions.

Both women are shown to have more significance than simply giving birth to the eponymous ancestors of Israel. In having the courage to disown their powerful father, they allow Jacob to return to Canaan. Thus, they are instrumental in actualizing the promises given to their people by God. In a striking display of strength and cleverness, Rachel is shown to outwit Laban and humiliate his gods. Her success, although unrecognized by Jacob, prompts him to stand up to Laban and finally reach a peaceful settlement that ensures the entire family's safety. Once in Canaan, the narrator does not discuss them, except for Rachel's death. Nonetheless, their contentiousness, due to the manipulation by Laban and the favoritism of Jacob, has its legacy in the parallel experiences of their children.

7

Dinah

The Fracturing
of a Tenuous Peace
in a Troubled Land

The narratives concerning Sarah, Rebekah, Rachel, and Leah have shown how crucial these women are for the continuation of God's promise of descendants. The narrator presents them in a way that emphasizes their participation in the promise first given to Abraham. Dinah is the first Israelite woman in Genesis who is neither a wife of one of the patriarchs nor a foreigner, but rather a member of the covenantal group as the daughter of Leah and Jacob.[1] Mention of Dinah is found only in the narrative in Genesis 34 that describes Shechem's assault upon her and its consequences.[2] Although her appearance is brief and her characterization elusive, her legacy is significant. This daughter of Israel illustrates the fragile nature of the promise of descendants, and also of the equally important promise of land.[3] Her story compels its readers to conclude that the promise of land is important not only for its own sake, but is also critical to the survival of the people of Israel, who are struggling to develop and maintain their own value system independent of the Canaanite way of life.

Interpreting this narrative is fraught with difficulties. As the account unfolds, there is a rapid increase in violence and bloodshed, there are many ambiguities of motivation in the text, and the perspective of the victim is never given. Dinah, an innocent woman, is sexually assaulted, yet the perpetrator of the violence comes to love her and wants to marry her. Does she remain at Shechem's house because she is forced to, or because she chooses to stay? Is Shechem sincere in his professed love? Shechem, who proposes to marry Dinah, stands outside the covenantal promise—he is a Hivite. Dinah's brothers do not accept Shechem's proposal, yet they pretend to do so. What motivates the Hivites to accept circumcision as terms for the marriage? The brothers of Dinah long for vengeance, yet in exacting it an entire city is destroyed. Jacob, Dinah's father, appears enigmatic. Does Jacob's silence indicate a flagrant disregard for his daughter's welfare, or a careful weighing of the potential political consequences of provoking war with the Hivites? Where should the reader's sentiments lie when the account ends? Dinah's own thoughts and feelings are never discussed. The narrator relates what happens to her and what actions are taken on her behalf, but the narrator neither comments on Dinah's reaction nor records any dialogue between her and the other people who appear in this account.

The confusion prompted by these questions, which ultimately are not given definitive answers by the narrator, is reflected in two recent studies. On the one hand, Dana Nolan Fewell and David M. Gunn argue that the moral judgment of the narrator is in fact revealed. A complicated ethical situation is presented, but the narrator "tips the balance" in Shechem's favor and condemns the "gross disresponse" of the brothers who exact revenge.[4] On the other hand, Mishael Caspi argues that Shechem is shown to be duplicitous throughout his dealings with Dinah and her family; hence the narrator sees revenge by her brothers to be justified.[5] This range in interpretation actually points to the permanent ambiguity that the narrator has created in this account. By presenting the complexities of the situation between the family of Dinah and the family of Shechem, as well as by placing this narrative in the context of Jacob's struggles in the land, the narrator compels the reader to reflect upon the precarious nature of the promise of land and descendants to the Israelites.

The Context: the Encounter of Jacob and Esau (Genesis 33:1-18)

Because the account of Dinah and Shechem is concerned with the violence that threatens not only Dinah herself but also the peace between the Israelites and Canaanites, it is appropriate to evaluate such an account in its context.[6] Indeed, the accounts, which immediately precede and follow the story of Dinah, are about the fragile coexistence of the people of Jacob and the people of Hamor and Shechem in the land that Jacob finds upon his return from Paddan-aram.[7]

It is appropriate to first examine Jacob's ominous encounter with Esau. Because Jacob returns to the land with all of his wives, concubines, and children, he is highly vulnerable. How can he defend such a large contingent of dependents? Moreover, the entire family could be destroyed and the promise to Abraham thus effectively annulled by a successful attack. Indeed, when Jacob and his family encounter him, Esau is accompanied by his army of four hundred men.

Up to this point in the Genesis narrative, Jacob has survived various troubles by his skill in using deception. Laban tricked him into marrying Leah, but he obtained his beloved Rachel as his wife as well. Laban's deceitful practices plagued Jacob throughout the length of his service, yet Jacob outwitted his father-in-law in the end. Moreover, Jacob was blessed with numerous children. Both of his wives, as well as their maids, provided him with eleven sons and a daughter. The sons, along with Benjamin, who is born later, become the progenitors of the twelve tribes of Israel. Having escaped servitude under Laban, Jacob finally returns to Canaan, the land of the promise. Until Jacob's return to Canaan, God's promise to Abraham of many descendants is incomplete; his children would be threatened as long as they live in a foreign land. Thus, the promises of descendants and of land are inextricably linked.

Jacob's past successes despite adversity set the stage for his reentry into Canaan. Will Jacob be safe when he encounters the brother who once vowed to kill him? Will Esau still be intent on killing Jacob? The introduction to the encounter at first appears ominous. The narrator appropriately reveals the scene through Jacob's eyes: "And Jacob lifted up his eyes and looked, and behold, Esau was coming, and four hundred men with him!" (33:1 RSV). Jacob could not defend his family and the entourage against four hundred men. His response reveals his primary preference for Rachel and her child and his secondary preference for Leah and her children over Zilpah, Bilhah, and their offspring. Thus, he exposes the servants and their children to perceived danger by placing them in front of his caravan, while he moves Leah, Rachel, and their children to the rear. Rachel and her child, Joseph, are the most protected.

Despite the threatening beginning, Jacob encounters a surprisingly conciliatory Esau. In contrast to Jacob, who assumes an obeisant posture by bowing to Esau, Esau unexpectedly runs in haste to meet his brother. The story takes a dramatic turn. The narrator informs the reader in four distinct phrases that Esau has had a change of heart. He not only "ran to meet him," but also "embraced him," "fell on his neck," and "kissed him" (33:4 RSV). The narrator stresses the emotional response of both men by revealing that "they wept" (33:4 RSV).[8] In recording that Esau spots

Jacob's numerous children, the narrator underscores the actualization of the promise of descendants. Jacob's first words to Esau relate that the children he sees were given by God (33:5), and thus the reader is reminded that they are the fruits of God's promise. Still in Esau's debt, Jacob calls himself Esau's "servant," and all of his maids, wives, and children bow down to Esau. Jacob offers a present to Esau, and after Esau's initial refusal, Jacob continues to press him to accept.[9] The narrator assures the reader of Esau's trust in his brother when he finally accepts the gift.

In contrast to Esau's acceptance of Jacob's gift, Jacob refuses to accept Esau's offerings. Esau asks Jacob to accompany him, but Jacob wants to keep his distance. Skilled in deception, he is not forthright about his intentions to permanently remain at a distance from Esau. Jacob first tells Esau that he cannot risk over-driving the flocks and herds, but he deferentially promises his "lord" that he will meet him in Seir. Esau counters by suggesting that some of his men remain with Jacob. Jacob refuses but the two brothers depart amicably. While Jacob conceals his plans to travel in another direction, the narrator relates, "So Esau returned that day on his way to Seir. But Jacob journeyed to Succoth, and built himself a house, and made booths for his cattle" (33:16-17 RSV).[10] Jacob avoided physical conflict with Esau and instead used quiet deception to keep their families apart.[11]

The account of the meeting of Jacob and Esau intimated potential violence, but conflict was averted by Esau's genuine graciousness and Jacob's deceptive compliance. Yet as the account continues, the conflict is not actually resolved; rather, it is only delayed. Ultimately, Jacob and Esau can never trust each other, nor can their descendants. It is not surprising, therefore, that as Jacob continues to encounter other Canaanite peoples, he finds strife. Jacob's temporary peace in Succoth will not continue.

Jacob's Arrival at Shechem (Gen. 33:18-20)

As Jacob's journeys in Canaan continue, he arrives at Shechem, the city inhabited by the sons of Hamor, including the son who bears the city's name. The fact that Jacob arrives there "safely" or "at peace" belies what occurs next (33:18).[12] Just as the reader expects violence but surprisingly finds peace when Jacob meets Esau, the reader expects peace at Shechem, but instead finds violence. In contrast to erecting a house, as he had done in Succoth, Jacob now pitches a tent, a temporary dwelling. Although he pays for the land, it appears uncertain whether the tent will be superseded by a permanent dwelling, or whether Jacob will need to move away from this city.

The identities of the men who sell the land to Jacob provide a clue to the importance of the interlude at Shechem. The reader is told that Jacob bought the land from "the sons of Hamor, the father of Shechem" (33:19), immediately drawing attention to this son Shechem. Who is this man and why is he singled out?

Shechem's Encounter with Dinah: Rape and Change of Heart (Gen. 34:1-4)

Although the entirety of the narrative is concerned with the rape of Dinah and the subsequent events, Dinah herself never figures prominently. Shechem rapes her, Hamor deceitfully misrepresents her situation to her family, Jacob abandons her, and Simeon and Levi both take extreme measures without consulting her. Dinah is treated as an object throughout these incidents; her own reaction to them is not recorded.

As the account begins, the narrator identifies Dinah as the daughter of Leah, and secondly, that Leah bore her to Jacob (34:1). By this identification, the reader is reminded that Dinah was born to the woman whom Jacob did not favor. The narrator previously has shown that Jacob gave the greatest protection to Rachel and her child when he feared the encounter with Esau might be violent. The reader is now led to wonder if Jacob will ignore Dinah as he did Leah. Will Dinah live as neglected an existence as did her mother?

Dinah, taking the initiative to leave the area that Jacob had purchased for his tent, is shown to visit some of the local women. This glimpse shows us that she acted independently, on her own initiative, perhaps encouraged by Jacob's lack of concern for her.[13] Given the problems with the Canaanites as well as the polemic against them, the narrator might also be suggesting that her decision was not wise. Nonetheless, it is important to note that Dinah was only visiting the *women* of the land—she was not trying to put herself in any position to encounter the men of the land or to marry a Canaanite. By giving us this detail, the narrator encourages the reader to be open-minded about her motivation.

At this point the action quickens. The narrator never relates whether Dinah reached her destination or that she encountered any Canaanite women. As soon as Shechem sees her, he attacks. The pace of the narrative emphasizes the violence that Shechem perpetrates against Dinah. Shechem is identified as the son of Hamor, the Hivite prince. Since the son of the prince acts so treacherously, the prince himself is suspect, as is the entire people. A series of three verbs underscores his violent move: "He took her and lay her and mishandled her" (34:2).[14] Unexpectedly, however, Shechem reverses his posture toward her. The next sentence immediately declares that he has a change of heart.[15] As abruptly as he had attacked her, Shechem asserts that he loves her. The omniscient narrator, in order to make this development credible, tells us Shechem's feelings instead of using Shechem's own words, which would be suspect.[16] The narrator states, "His soul was drawn to Dinah, the daughter of Jacob, and he loved the maiden and he spoke to the heart of the maiden" (34:3).[17] Shechem asks his father, Hamor, to advise him about his newly found love. It is already known that Hamor is the prince of the region and that Jacob has bought from him the land on which he currently dwells. Hamor clearly has power over Jacob. Shechem makes a startling request of his father—he asks him to obtain Dinah to be his wife. Shechem has already said that he loves Dinah and he speaks tenderly to her, yet the words he uses to his father are blunt. He tells his father, "Take this girl for me to be my wife" (34:4). He does not refer to Dinah by name and calls her "girl" *(yaldâ)* instead of the more respectful "maiden" *(na῾ărā)*, as he does when he addresses her family (34:12) and as the narrator refers to her (34:3). Not only did Shechem "take" *(yiqqaḥ)* Dinah when he assaulted her (34:2), but he also demands that his father again "take" *(qaḥ)* her (34:4). Shechem, her assailant, who comes from a rival group, wants to marry her. Surprisingly, Hamor does not respond to his son's demanding tone, indicating that Shechem is more powerful than his father in this scene. He makes demands of his father, and his father has no response.

The Appeal of Shechem and Hamor to Dinah's Family (34:5-12)

Jacob is informed of his daughter's fate before the Hivites can state their case. Dinah is now identified solely as Jacob's daughter (34:5, 7), pointing to his significance for her future. The reader now ponders how Jacob will respond to his daughter's attacker.

Surprisingly, Jacob does not immediately respond to the assault. Does his hesitation necessarily mean that he is not concerned about his daughter? Does he disregard Dinah because she is Leah's daughter? Or is it possible that his hesitation arises from the precarious situation? Might Jacob fear a more serious confrontation? Jacob knows that Hamor's sons, who sold him the land, operate from a position of economic and military strength.

His previous encounter with Esau has revealed his fear and his decision to use deception to avoid further encounters. Ultimately several possible motives remain in tension in the reader's mind.[18] The narrator suggests the possibilities by the context but does not resolve this ambiguity.

The response to the conflict now shifts to the second generation, the sons of Hamor and the sons of Jacob.[19] The narrator indicates this first by having Jacob wait for his sons to return from the fields. Indeed, it will be the sons alone who carry out the revenge. Not only does Jacob himself hear of the assault from sources unknown to us, but so too do the brothers hear of it from unspecified sources. The crime has now become public and the entirety of the two communities is now involved. The text is ambiguous as to whether they learn of the crime against Dinah before or after they return home. Verse 7a may be translated either, "Jacob's sons came from the field when they heard about it, and the men were grieved and very angry"; or, "Jacob's sons came from the field; when they heard about it, the men were grieved and very angry."[20] By the use of these emphatic phrases, the narrator underscores the brothers' pain and anger and allows the reader to sympathize with them. The word used for "grieve" (yit‘aṣṣēbû) is also used to indicate God's grief concerning the state of humanity before the flood (6:6). Moreover, the word for "angry" (yiḥar) is used to describe God's anger against those who would afflict the widow or the orphan (Exod. 22:23), or against Balaam when he journeyed to meet Balak in order to curse Israel (Num. 22:22).

Before Jacob or his sons can express their anger, Hamor speaks. He neither apologizes for Shechem's attack on Dinah, expresses remorse, nor comments on her welfare.[21] Rather, Hamor immediately asks Jacob to give Dinah to Shechem in marriage. Surprisingly, this is not the only issue that concerns him. He further attempts to use the incident to introduce a new policy, suggesting that his people and Jacob's people intermarry. The assault on and request of marriage to one Israelite by one Hivite becomes the catalyst for the request of the Hivites to have access to all Israelite women.[22] Hamor presents his request as a reasonable policy: the two groups will live together as one. This policy will be part of a new relationship between the two groups of peoples—they would now live, work, trade, and dwell together.

Before Jacob can respond, Shechem interrupts to add that he will give whatever gift they request of him. Moreover, like his father, Shechem does not admit that he raped Dinah. He again pleads intensely for Dinah to be given as his wife. This scene recalls the encounter of Esau and Jacob and the offering to exchange gifts. Will Shechem's gift ultimately be refused, as was Esau's? His tone is respectful, referring to Dinah as "maiden" *(naʿărā)*, and he begins his words with the polite address, "Let me find favor in your eyes." Thus, two perspectives are kept in tension in this scene. Hamor's view stresses the expectation for future linkages between the peoples, whereas Shechem's view underscores his desperation for Dinah. By retaining both motivations for the marriage between Shechem and Dinah, the narrator encourages the reader to consider the complexity of the situation without passing immediate judgment.

The Response of Jacob's Sons (Gen. 34:13-17)

The deceit so often practiced by the characters of the Book of Genesis again predominates. Jacob, who deceived his father and uncle, now has sons who act in the same manner. Rather than confront Hamor and Shechem about the rape, they pretend to be amicable. The narrator is forthright about the motive for their deceit, however. He states that they plot against the Hivites because Shechem "had defiled their sister Dinah" (34:13 RSV). Their deception of the Shechemites is balanced by the sympathetic description of their motivation. But by retaining this complexity of the action, the narrator continues to force the reader to remain conscious of the moral ambiguity of their actions.

The sons proceed with the plan. They state that any joining of the two peoples must be done on their terms; the Hivites must be circumcised.[23] Since circumcision is the sign of the covenant, the issue at stake is not only Dinah's welfare, but also the integrity of the entire nascent Israelite community. Would the intermarriage of the Hivites and Israelites threaten the promise of land or the promise of descendants?[24] Was giving Dinah to one who is uncircumcised and thus not a member of the covenant a "disgrace"? Because Dinah already has been abused, the narrator suggests that, from her brothers' perspective, the disgrace has already occurred. The importance of the covenantal promises of land and descendants is again implied when Jacob's sons state to the Hivites that if they would only become circumcised, "we will dwell with you and become one people" (34:16 RSV). The reader knows that because an uncircumcised man already violated Dinah, the gulf between the two peoples has grown. Throughout this section Jacob neither participates nor responds to the sons' demands. Indeed, the sons take over the responsibilities of their father. By the absence of his comments, it is difficult for the reader to come to a conclusion about the merits of the sons' suggestions.

The Response of the Hivites (Gen. 34:18-24)

Because of the extreme demands made on the Hivites by Jacob's sons, it seems surprising that Hamor and Shechem are content to receive them. At first the narrator presents Shechem's feelings positively; he is pleased solely because of his feelings for Dinah. However, when Shechem addresses the men of the village, he appeals to broader concerns. He states that Jacob's people are friendly and that they would be valuable trading partners. To preempt any impending objection, he states, "Will not their cattle, their property and all their beasts be ours?" (34:23 RSV). At this point, a motivation outside of love for Dinah lies behind his plan. Because of his need to convince his townspeople, however, the reader is not persuaded to dismiss his love for Dinah. Is he being practical, and in fact, clever, in his approach to his people? Or do his economic interests supersede his love for Dinah? These questions are left unresolved. The problem is, in fact, compounded by the fact that when the men of the city agree to be circumcised, they know nothing of the covenant but agree for economic reasons alone.[25]

The Execution of Revenge (Gen. 34:25-29)

Although all of the brothers acted deceitfully in suggesting the circumcision, Simeon and Levi initiate the slaughter.[26] By stating that these two men are "Dinah's brothers," the narrator indicates that they are her full brothers, the sons of Leah and Jacob, and thereby feel the indignity with greater resentment. They wait until the third day after the circumcision to carry out their revenge, a time when the Hivites will be less suspicious of an attack, yet still are recovering. A separate phrase announces that Hamor and Shechem are slain and that Dinah is taken out of Shechem's house.[27]

Dinah is still treated as an object. Initially, she was attacked by Shechem against her will, and now she is taken away from her new home by her brothers, who do not ask her about her wishes.[28] The narrator does not specify if she considers Shechem her enemy or her beloved betrothed, and her brothers do not attempt to discover. The narrator's audience would be familiar with the legislation that says an unmarried woman, if raped, was to be married by the rapist and could not be divorced—a custom that was to protect her from being ineligible as a marriage candidate.[29] Thus, the brothers' actions are unfair to Dinah. The revenge does not end with the slaughter by Simeon and Levi; the rest of Jacob's sons come to plunder the city and take the wives and children as prey. It is ironic that although

Shechem had told the men of the city that all the goods of the Israelites would be theirs, the reverse has occurred.

Jacob's Response (Gen. 34:30-31)

The narrator appropriately raises the reader's questioning of the extreme measure Dinah's brothers have taken by finally revealing Jacob's perspective. Although the Hivites are now dead, he argues, the Canaanites and Perizzites will now be greater enemies. Jacob rightly laments, "I am few in number" (34:30).[30] Although Jacob and his family were threatened by the actions of the Shechemites against Dinah, the response by Jacob's sons has not helped their situation. The covenantal promise continues to be threatened by outside forces.[31] The account of Dinah's attack and its aftermath demonstrates that Jacob's concern for the future of the family's welfare is legitimate.

Continuing Problems in the Land (Gen. 35:1-15)

The account of the rape of Dinah is surrounded by narratives about problems in the land with the Canaanites. The initial threat to Jacob was from Esau. After the struggle with the Hivites, however, further potential threats exist.

Following the Dinah narrative, God tells Jacob to travel to Bethel "and make there an altar to the God who appeared to you when you fled from your brother Esau" (35:1 RSV). Although the reference is to Jacob's strife with Esau when they were youths (chapter 28), it also recalls Jacob's more recent experience upon encountering Esau. This sets the stage for the new journey where Jacob will face additional threats from people in the land. Before he begins to complete God's command to journey to Bethel, he first purges all idols from among his own people, and, notably, "concealed them under the oak which was near Shechem" (35:4). The city of Shechem, already associated with the crime against Dinah, now becomes associated with a depository for idols as well.

God's providence protects Jacob again, and the people of the land do not dare attack him and his family (35:5). The text states, "A terror from God fell upon the cities that were round about them, so that they did not pursue the sons of Jacob" (35:5 RSV). This "terror," part of the language of Holy War, refers to the inability of peoples to attack Israel because of God's intervention.[32] The Divine Warrior protects the Israelites throughout their history. Indeed, after Jacob's safe arrival, the promise of land and descendants is reiterated: "The land which I gave to Abraham and Isaac I will give to you, and I will give the land to your descendants after you" (35:12 RSV). The tangible confirmation of the promise comes immediately after Jacob's safe arrival in Bethel, when Benjamin, the progenitor of the tribe of the monarchy, is born to Rachel.

Conclusions

By placing the account of Dinah in context, it can be seen that her story is used to demonstrate that the promise of God for land and descendants is, at times, in doubt. Dinah suffered innocently because of the danger that lay in a land dominated by Canaanites. From the narrator's comprehensive examination of all angles of this event, it is clear that the Hivites suffered as well when Jacob's sons took revenge. Moreover, Dinah is not the first woman to suffer because of a foreigner's strength and her protectors' weaknesses: Sarah and Rebekah were placed in danger because of Pharaoh's and Abimelech's dominance and Abraham's and Isaac's cowardice.

This narrative deals with a situation that is not easy to adjudicate. The initial crime is severe and the rape is condemned. Yet, once revenge is sought, it seems to go too far; all the Hivite males are killed, and their wives, children, and property are taken. How does the narrator judge such a situation? The complexities are carefully shown. The narrator knows that the crime against Dinah was wrong, and the fact that Shechem truly loved Dinah after the assault occurred is not hidden—yet it never justified the violence done to her. The narrator recognizes that Dinah's brothers were properly motivated to avenge their sister, but the fact that Jacob becomes further threatened because of potential Canaanite reprisals shows that the revenge led to an even more threatening situation. By skillfully presenting these views and nuances, the narrator succeeds in showing us many aspects of this crime and its repercussions.

By maintaining these ambiguities and complexities, the narrator challenges the reader to consider both the Israelites and the Hivites as human beings and not simplistically as caricatures. In the final analysis, this narrative provides one of the best cases of unresolved ambiguity. The narrator has chosen this means to preserve a nuanced reflection on what is seen to be a difficult episode in early Israel's experience.

8

Tamar

The Woman
Who Demanded Justice

Powerless members of society who are wronged cannot always confront the perpetrators of injustice. The society in which they live may ignore the poor, exclude the aliens, or oppress minorities, and the rich or powerful may retaliate against any who complain or confront them. Because the women represented in the Book of Genesis are all less powerful than the men in their society, many of them must resort to nonconfrontational methods of dealing with the injustices they experience. Hagar flees when Sarah and Abraham mistreat her, and eventually she makes a new life for herself in her homeland. The daughters of Lot, prevented by their father from finding husbands, have children by him. Leah, denied Jacob's love, takes comfort in the many children given to her by God.

The story of Tamar (38:1-30) portrays a childless widow wronged by two men, Onan, her brother-in-law, and Judah, her father-in-law. After Tamar's husband Er dies, Onan is required by law to have intercourse with her and to marry her in order that she may have a child and that she might continue to be supported. Onan spurns his obligations to Tamar and is subsequently slain by God. Judah also casts her aside and refuses to give his youngest son, Shelah, to her in marriage. How does Tamar respond to these inequities? At first she does not confront her father-in-law, but later she carefully constructs a plan to have children of the line of Judah—from

Judah himself. By disguising herself as a prostitute, Judah has sexual relations with her through which she becomes pregnant. Tamar's plan ostensibly protects her honor; if she eventually must face Judah or if she is charged with prostitution, she will reveal evidence against him. When her life is directly threatened because of Judah's cruelty, she courageously confronts him and is justified.

The Context: Judah's Participation in Joseph's Anguish (Gen. 37:25-36)

The story of Tamar is found within the lengthy narrative of the intrigue against Joseph, his rise to power in Egypt, and his protection of his brothers (Genesis 37–50).[1]

Judah's behavior and character are the subject of the chapter that immediately precedes the account of Tamar. The sons of Jacob have plotted against their brother Joseph. First they agree to kill him, but when Reuben urges them to spare his life, the brothers proceed with Reuben's plan to gain their father's debt and appreciation through a staged rescue of Joseph. The text implies that all the brothers except for Reuben cast Joseph in a pit, and that Reuben would later save him (37:22; cf. 38:29, 30).

Judah, however, has his own plan. Perhaps these multiple plans indicate that originally there circulated two alternate accounts to explain why Joseph was not killed. Nevertheless, in the current structure of the story, they must be interpreted as sequential scenes. Judah proposes that Joseph be sold for profit. The narrator reveals Judah as a scheming and corrupt man. He is able to convince his brothers by contrasting his proposed crime to the murder that the brothers originally planned and by remaining silent about Reuben's plan, which already has been accepted. Moreover, he tries to conceal that his plan would result in a worse fate for Joseph than Reuben's proposal.

Judah's hope for gain in this intrigue is repeatedly emphasized by the narrator. For example, the description of the Ishmaelite traders is not miscellaneous information; their wealth prompts Judah's plot. Their camels alone indicate wealth, but they also are loaded with "gum, balm, and myrrh" (37:25 RSV). Upon seeing them Judah articulates his scheme. At first he is candid about the gain to be made, stating, "What profit is it if we slay our brother and conceal his blood?" (37:26 RSV). However, the reader already knows that Joseph's brothers are no longer considering murder. Indeed, before Judah spoke, all were seated and eating, awaiting

Reuben's return. Judah's pleas for Joseph's life are a transparent deception for distraction from his true motive: personal gain.

The narrator clearly considers Judah's plan to be more harsh than the alternative suggested by Reuben and initially carried out by the brothers. The narrator contrasts the two plans by having Reuben absent when Judah reveals the details to his brothers and when his suggestion is carried out. Indeed, when Reuben returns and discovers that Joseph has already been sold, he rends his garments, a sign of mourning or repentance, and cries in anguish. Moreover, Judah's crime leads to yet another. By staining Joseph's coat with the blood of a goat, the brothers trick their father into believing that Joseph has suffered a horrible death—he has been devoured by a wild beast. Jacob remains inconsolable.

Judah's Life among the Canaanites: Marriage and Birth of His Sons (Gen. 38:1-5)

After having determined Joseph's fate, Judah continues his questionable behavior. He leaves his brothers and his father and travels into Canaanite territory. There he "turned aside to an Adullamite man, whose name was Hirah" (38:1). The word used for "turned aside" (*wayyēṭ*) may also be used figuratively to indicate deviating from what is right or to indicate disloyalty.[2] The narrator thereby suggests that Judah's political loyalties are leaning in the direction of this Canaanite man.[3] Like his uncle Esau, Judah distances himself from his own people by marrying a Canaanite woman, the unnamed daughter of Shua.[4] The pace of the narrative moves very quickly from this point since its primary importance is to inform us about the sons of this marriage. Their union is fertile; without any difficulty, three sons are born.[5]

The names of the sons, Er, Onan, and Shelah, are significant. The root *ʿwr*, from which Er derives, can mean "to rouse oneself" or "to be exposed/bare," and the word *ʿwr*, which sounds similar to Er *(ʿēr)*, means "skin." Onan, which comes from the root *ʿwn* ("be at rest"), means "vigorous." The meanings of these names are appropriate and ironic. Er, who is slain by God for an unrecorded sin, is indeed "exposed." Onan, who refuses to be "vigorous" with Tamar (and does not enjoy a life of rest) also is slain. Shelah, which comes from the root *šlh*, meaning "to be quiet," remains a silent and inactive character in the narrative. These children appear to have inherited Canaanite values, frequently portrayed by the Israelites as inherently immoral. Thus, the deaths of Er and Onan, killed by God because of their sinful disobedience, come as no surprise.

Introduction of Tamar and
Her Life with Judah's Family (Gen. 38:1-11)

Tamar becomes a part of Judah's family when he obtains her as a wife for his son, Er. Nothing is known about this woman except her name, which means "palm tree." Her name, however, is significant, for although she will be fertile neither in her union with Er nor with Onan, her offspring eventually will comprise the Israelite tribe that will provide the Davidic line of kings. Although Tamar's origins are not stated, the narrator suggests that she is a Canaanite because it is not specified that Judah went back to his own family or land for a wife.[6] The depiction of Tamar as a righteous woman mitigates the denigration of the other Canaanites who feature in Judah's life. By leaving the issue ambiguous, however, the narrator may allow for greater acceptance of the woman who will become the ancestress of the Davidic line.

Judah's character and life among the Canaanites appears negatively to influence his first son Er. Er's crimes are not specified, but he "was evil" in God's sight and God "killed him" (38:7).[7]

Although Judah lives among the Canaanites, he does not renounce his origins. He remembers the law of the levirate marriage, wherein a brother is required to marry the widow of his dead sibling and have a child with her in the name of the dead brother so that his descendants might continue. Judah alludes to this law when he states to his second son Onan: "Go to your brother's wife and perform the brother-in-law's duty to her, and raise up offspring for your brother" (38:8). The word that is translated "and perform the brother-in-law's duty" (wĕyabbēm) is found in Deut. 25:5,7, where it specifically refers to the levirate marriage.[8] The marriage not only provided descendants for the deceased man, but also provided a marriage and support for a woman who was now an anomaly in society.[9]

Although the narrator presents Judah as a man who is aware of the custom concerning widows and the levirate marriage, Judah does not specify the totality of these obligations to his son Onan. Eschewing the obligation of marriage, and thus any responsibility for Tamar, he tells his son to have sexual intercourse and father a child, but he does not specify that Onan should marry Tamar. Indeed, he expresses no concern for his daughter-in-law, who now has no means of support.

Like his brother Er, Onan is a reprehensible man. His greed and disrespect for his brother and for Tamar prompt him to inflict more wounds upon her. First she is widowed and then she is denied care by her father-in-law. She is not only denied Onan in marriage, her right to have children by him also is withheld. Onan is particularly odious in the way he denies her the possibility of becoming pregnant. He does not refuse to lie with her. Rather, he exploits her trust and pretends to fulfill his duty. He repeatedly goes to her, takes advantage of her sexually, reaches sexual climax, yet "whenever he came into his brother's wife, he destroyed (it— i.e., his semen) on the ground" (38:9). The choice of *šíḥēt* (destroyed) underscores Onan's selfish exploitation because it connotes corruption and ruin.[10] There is no doubt in the narrator's mind that Onan, like Er, is utterly corrupt; the narrator comments that God judged this act and killed him (38:10).

Like his son, Onan, Judah pretends to have Tamar's interest at heart when in reality he perpetrates another injustice upon her. Instead of caring for her in his own home, he tells her to wait in her father's house until his son Shelah "grows up" (38:11 RSV), implying that Shelah will fulfill the levirate duty to her. The narrator suggests Judah's duplicity with this reference because his words specify neither marriage nor sexual union. It is surprising that he sends her to her father's house because the expected place of her residence would be to remain with him.[11] Judah fears that Shelah might be killed in Tamar's company, as were Er and Onan. But he is also impetuous and does not inquire of Tamar what transpired.[12]

Tamar's plight is subtly contrasted with Judah's situation and obligation by the narrator's choice of words. When Judah addresses Tamar, the narrator reminds us that she is "his daughter-in-law" (38:11). Moreover, when Judah speaks of Shelah, he pointedly calls him "my son." Judah, who fears losing this son, ignores Tamar's right to ever have one.

Tamar's thoughts and response to Judah are not recorded. Her actions tell us that she was obedient, even in the face of this injustice. Her response belies her strength, which will be revealed in the next episode.

Tamar's Plan (Gen. 38:12-14)

In parallel to his daughter-in-law's experience, Judah too discovers that he is bereft of a spouse. After his mourning period ends, however, he fails to reconsider giving Shelah to Tamar. Instead, he continues with the routine of his daily life and goes to the sheepshearers at Timnah with Hirah, the Adullamite, who is now identified as his friend or fellow citizen *(rēʿēhû)*. The connotation of "the fellow citizen" (38:12) is most appropriate here because Judah shuns his Israelite inheritance by rejecting his obligations to Tamar.

Tamar discovers from unidentified sources that Judah has plans to travel to Timnah. This time her feelings are revealed by the omniscient narrator, who leaves no doubt that Judah is responsible for unjustly keeping her a childless widow. The narrator states, "She saw that Shelah was grown up, and she had not been given to him as a wife" (38:14). Indeed, the narrator knows that not only should Shelah be sexually united with her in order that she might have a child, but also that he is obliged to marry her. Tamar does not confront Judah, but she does act decisively and ingeniously. She "put off her widow's garments, and wore a veil, wrapping herself up, and sat at the entrance to Enaim" (38:14).[13]

Judah's Encounter with Tamar (Gen. 38:15-19)

Tamar's plan at first proceeds without difficulty. She does nothing to prompt Judah; she merely sits at the roadside. Judah presumes she is a prostitute because of the way she has disguised herself. The narrator reveals twice that "he thought her to be a harlot, for she had covered her face" (38:15 RSV), and "he did not know that she was his daughter-in-law" (38:16 RSV). By referring to Tamar as Judah's daughter-in-law instead of by her proper name, the narrator hints at her upcoming relationship to Judah as a sexual partner because *kallâ* may mean either "daughter-in-law" or "bride." It is striking that not only does Judah fail to recognize her because of her dress, he does not guess her identity even after he speaks with her. This demonstrates how little Judah knew her and how long it had been since he inquired of her.

When Judah sees her, he immediately asks to lie with her. His language is direct: "Please come, I will come into you" (38:16). She responds prudently in order to obviate any charge of wrongdoing. In a series of pointed exchanges, she establishes the price and the pledge to pay it. Judah offers to send her a kid, a reasonable price for him, because he is on his way to Timnah where his flock is being sheared. However, Tamar knows better than to trust the word of such a duplicitous man. She demands a pledge. When Judah hesitates to specify the pledge, Tamar seizes the opportunity to define it: the signet, cord, and staff that could unmistakenly identify the man who lay with her. In this dialogue, Judah appears indecisive and lustful whereas Tamar appears skillful and prudent.

Judah, who had quickly impregnated his own wife, immediately impregnates Tamar as well. The father unwittingly accomplishes what Er was unable to do and what Onan was unwilling to do. The immediacy of her pregnancy is a startling reversal to the injustice done to her. Tamar's innocence as a prostitute is revealed by the narrator's final comment on this scene. Tamar does not attempt to remain as a prostitute for a moment. She immediately puts on the clothing that identifies her as a widow.[14]

Judah's Attempt to Retrieve His Pledge (Gen. 38:20-23)

Judah continues his association with his Canaanite friend, Hirah the Adullamite, and has him send the kid, the payment he had promised Tamar, to the place where he had encountered her. The narrator does not mention the name of this friend here but rather simply calls him "the Adullamite" (38:20), because what matters is not his name, but the fact that he is a Canaanite. It is significant that Judah's payment is a kid, since this term, *gĕdî*, which refers to the offspring of either a sheep or goat, recalls previous scenes in the narrative. Not only did Tamar begin her plan when she heard that Judah was traveling to shear his sheep, but the account that precedes the Tamar episode shows that Jacob was deceived into believing that Joseph was devoured by a wild beast because his coat was dipped into the blood of a goat by his brothers. Furthermore, the newly born offspring of the goat or sheep reminds us of the injustice done to Tamar by Judah—the withholding of offspring from her.

When Hirah, the Adullamite, arrives and does not find Tamar, he inquires of the men of the area. He refers to Tamar as the cult prostitute *(haqqĕdēšâ)* as opposed to a common prostitute *(zōnâ)* that was used earlier. These two types of prostitutes served different functions in Israelite society. The cult prostitute, either male or female, was severely condemned by religious authorities as a corrupt Canaanite practice, but the frequency with which it is condemned reveals its pervasiveness. Although common prostitutes carried social stigma, they were probably tolerated as long as they were not married women.[15] By the use of this term, the narrator suggests that Hirah presumes that Judah was participating in a characteristic Canaanite ritual activity.[16] Indeed, Judah was acting like a Canaanite in his relationship with Tamar. When Hirah reports his lack of success to Judah, Judah nonetheless holds that his obligation to "the prostitute" is over. In a clever use of irony, Hirah reports that the men of the village have told him that "no harlot *(qĕdēšâ)* has been here" (38:21). Indeed, the reader knows that Tamar is neither a cult prostitute nor a common prostitute, but a widow seeking her rights to have a child. Judah dismisses the necessity to pay Tamar when he tells Hirah that "the prostitute" may keep the pledge

and that Hirah's single attempt is sufficient. His only interest is his rep-
utation. He allows Tamar to keep the pledge lest he be scorned. He is not
concerned that his promise be kept. Thus, he himself does not attempt to
find her, nor does he consider sending Hirah again.[17]

The Discovery of Tamar's Pregnancy
(Gen. 38:24-26)

Judah learns of Tamar's pregnancy quickly—within three months. His
response is incredibly cruel; he not only assumes the role of deciding judge,
but he prescribes the harshest sentence, namely, death by burning. He
arrogantly proclaims the caustic sentence: "Take her out and let her be
burned" (38:24).[18] Death by burning is specified for the act of prostitution
by a priest's daughter (Lev. 21:9) and if a man takes a woman and her
mother as wives, all are to be punished this way (Lev. 20:14). But while
adultery is punishable by death, burning is not the usual sentence.[19] Moreover, in order for Tamar to be considered an adultress, she must be either
Er's widow or Shelah's future wife. Tamar has been denied on both accounts. As Er's widow, she was denied care and offspring. And Shelah
has been withheld from her by Judah.

Tamar's response to this injustice is to rely on the evidence she previously obtained from Judah. In two sentences she sends word to Judah
on the identity of the man who impregnated her. She begins by stating,
"By the man to whom these things belong, I am pregnant" (38:25). This
statement would be enough, but to underscore the tangible evidence, she
refers separately to each item and says, "Mark, please, whose these are,
the signet, and the cord, and the staff" (38:25). Tamar does not protest
her fate, but remains confident of the evidence she has provided. The reader
must now await the outcome anxiously. Might Judah deny that the objects
are his? Has Tamar's faith been misplaced or will Judah respond justly and
fairly to her?

To Judah's credit, he admits his parenthood. He immediately acknowledges the items, declares that he has wrongly denied Tamar his son,
Shelah, and says that she is more righteous than he. Tamar need no longer
fear for her life. His statement that he "did not give her to Shelah, my
son" (38:26) implies that not only did he not tell Shelah to have sexual
relations with her, but that he was wrong in not having Shelah marry her.
Tamar now is assured that she will continue her pregnancy and will have
descendants. However, the ending of the account shows us that she must

yet suffer another injustice. Judah does not offer Shelah to Tamar in marriage at this point. Although Tamar will no longer be a childless widow, she remains a widow denied the right of the levirate marriage. Although the text does not reflect further on the actions of Judah, it is clear that Tamar did not become Shelah's wife, as was her right. Judah acknowledges his unfairness to her, but makes no effort to rectify the injustice. There is no indication given that he will provide for this pregnant widow.

Conclusions

Tamar's experience of injustice is universal. It is impossible to live without seeing injustice in the world unless one chooses to ignore it. Once aware of injustice, one may demand rectification, but in many cases it persists. Frequently, injustice is only partially corrected. Tamar's own initiative enabled her to have the child to which she was entitled, but the reader knows that an injustice remains—Judah does not provide support for her. Tamar gives birth to the twins Perez and Zerah (38:27-30), and through Perez becomes one of the ancestors of David, but Judah's denial of Shelah to Tamar is a lingering injustice. Although the narrator does not directly comment on this situation, the plot engages our sympathies for Tamar because sensitive people can identify with her plight. As a woman under the authority of her father-in-law, Tamar was dependent on him for justice. When Judah deprived Tamar of her rights, her strength and courage enabled her to have a child, yet she was unable to overcome the injustice of being denied a husband.

Some will find this ending pessimistic, but it is also possible to see Tamar's experience as a model of courage in the face of terrible odds. Justice is not always accomplished in one's lifetime, but Tamar's partial success sustained her hope. Dissatisfaction can either paralyze people or encourage them to fight for what is rightfully theirs. Tamar, fueled by her own resolve to struggle for what she believed in, never gave up.

9

Potiphar's Wife
The Stereotyped Temptress

The previous chapters have described seven distinct portraits of women. Their sexuality was consistently emphasized in the portrayal of their importance. However, their ability to be someone's wife or to have children was never the sole criterion for their prominence. Although Sarah, Rebekah, Rachel, and Leah fulfilled God's plan for them to be the mothers of the promised descendants, they also participated in the crucial covenantal beginnings of Israel. They ensured, for example, that God's designated choices receive the significant blessings of their fathers, and in some cases they guaranteed the safety of their families. Although the narrative of Dinah does not develop her as an independent character, the account shows that the injustice done to her has repercussions for the relationship of the nascent people of Israel with its neighbors. The depictions of foreign women, namely, Lot's daughters, Hagar, and (possibly) Tamar, demonstrate that the narrator is sensitive to the dignity of foreign peoples. Lot's daughters do not commit incest out of depravity; they are led to believe they have no other choice because of the actions of their father. Hagar, an Egyptian, perceived to be an enemy by Sarah, is addressed by God who promises her a nation of descendants through her son. Tamar proves to be a more righteous person than her false accuser, Judah, the son of the patriarch Jacob. In all these narratives, complex portrayals of these women and their lives enable the reader to see them as more than sexual stereotypes.

The story of Joseph and Potiphar's wife, however, is a more simplistic narrative. Potiphar's wife is a caricature of the foreign temptress who tries to seduce the righteous Joseph. The narrator introduces the wife of Potiphar without much regard for development of character or complexity of motivation. Nonetheless, the narrative is used to further the course of Joseph's stay in Egypt with heightened dramatic import. Until Potiphar's wife is introduced, Joseph is ensconced in his position as assistant to the captain of Pharaoh's bodyguard. After this woman's false accusation and his subsequent imprisonment, Joseph actually rises to a higher station in Pharaoh's court and thus is strategically placed to save his brothers from famine.

The Narrative in Context (Gen. 37–38)

A previous narrative (37:1-36), separated by the account of Tamar and Judah, begins the Joseph cycle. This first episode details how Joseph's brothers sold him as a slave. The juxtaposition of the narrative of Tamar with the narrative of the attempted seduction of Joseph by Potiphar's wife encourages the reader to consider the relationship between the two accounts. Both deal with a woman's attempt to have sexual relations with a son of Jacob. Both women refer to the man's clothing as evidence of having been sexually approached. The contrast between these narratives, however, is striking. The story of Tamar portrays a righteous woman unjustly accused by Judah. The narrative of Potiphar's wife shows a deceitful woman with the virtuous Joseph.[1] Through this deliberate arrangement of texts, the narrator enables the reader to more fully contrast the circumstances and behavior of the characters.[2] Although Tamar is possibly a foreigner,[3] the narrator seems to highlight the increased risk that foreign women pose to Israelite men in the story of Potiphar's wife, especially when the men are in a distant land. The narrator suggests that under such circumstances of political domination by a foreign power, sexual liaisons with foreigners are apt to lead the faithful away from their traditions.[4] Joseph's refusal to have a sexual relationship with Potiphar's wife may be contrasted with Judah's readiness to approach Tamar. Joseph again stands apart from his brothers.

Introduction to Joseph's Circumstances in Egypt (Gen. 39:1-6a)

The first words of the introduction direct attention to the man who has ultimate power over Joseph—Potiphar. The first sentence appears overloaded with the multiplicity of parenthetical phrases used to describe him. Besides being identified by his proper name, he is cited as an "officer of

Pharaoh" *(serîs par<oh)*. His duties are further specified as "the captain of the guard" *(śar haṭṭabāhîm,* 39:1 RSV). The first description, although clearly indicating his official duties as an officer, also has the connotation of "eunuch."[5] The narrator thus creates an open question for the reader to consider. Was Potiphar a eunuch? If he were a eunuch, Potiphar's wife would have an additional reason to pursue a sexual liaison with Joseph.

This question of Potiphar's sexual identity is never answered by the narrator. Instead, the question takes on other dimensions because an additional character, Potiphara, whose name differs by only a single letter *(pôṭîpera<)*, is identified as being the father of the woman whom Joseph marries.[6] Is he the same man? The narrator never resolves these questions.[7]

Perhaps the additional identification of this man as an Egyptian was originally used in place of the proper name, Potiphar, but in the current context where his name has already been specified, it calls attention to his nationality.[8] He is a man of privilege and station, whereas Joseph is a slave, whom Potiphar purchased from the Ishmaelites. The descendants of Ishmael, the son of Hagar who was once forced to leave Canaan, have now become the catalysts for removing Joseph, a descendant of Isaac, to the land of Ishmael's refuge.

Although Joseph is controlled by this powerful Egyptian, the narrator indicates immediately that because Joseph enjoys God's favor and protection he becomes successful. More striking is the narrator's report that Potiphar is aware that the God of Israel is with Joseph and causes him to prosper. The reader is left with the impression that although Potiphar is Joseph's master, he nonetheless acknowledges the God of Israel as Joseph's protector. Therefore, when Joseph is later falsely accused by Potiphar's wife, the reader's fear that Potiphar might use the severest punishment is mitigated by the knowledge that he is a man who seems to fear Joseph's God.

By using a multiplicity of phrases and references, the narrator stresses that Potiphar completely trusted Joseph with his household affairs, and that God blessed Joseph and his master's household. The narrator presents an adequate case for this conclusion: Potiphar "did not trouble himself about anything except the food that he ate" (39:6).[9]

Introduction to Potiphar's Wife (Gen. 39:6b-10)

The narrator does not let the reader rest content with the knowledge of Joseph's comforts alone. The narrator introduces a detail about Joseph that at first appears to have no connection to the information given previously: "Joseph was beautiful in form and beautiful to look at" *(wayehî yôsēp yĕpēh-tōʾar wîpēh marʾeh,* 39:6). This expression reflects the description of Sarah and Rachel.[10] The reader recalls that Abraham's assessment of Sarah's beauty led to her endangerment and that Jacob's immediate love for Rachel was complicated by her father and sister. By recalling these incidents, the narrator encourages us to surmise that Joseph is in danger. At the same time, the phrase hints of the future rise in stature that Joseph will gain after his false imprisonment. While in prison for allegedly attacking Potiphar's wife, Joseph interprets Pharaoh's dream of the robust and emaciated cows that signify the forthcoming years of plenty and famine. The cows, which signify prosperity, are also described as "beautiful to look at" *(yĕpōt marʾeh,* 41:2, 4) and "beautiful in form" *(yîpōt tōʾar,* 41:18).

The significance of Joseph's appearance becomes clear with the introduction of Potiphar's wife. Throughout the account, the narrator never uses the woman's name, referring to her instead as either "his [Joseph's] master's wife" (39:7, 8) or "his [Potiphar's] wife" (39:9, 19). In this first instance where she is introduced, the term "his master's wife" not only emphasizes her status as a married woman with authority over servants, but also as the woman whose husband has control of Joseph's very life. Just as Jacob was enamored with Rachel's beauty when he first saw her (29:10-11), so too does Potiphar's wife look upon Joseph (39:7). Potiphar's wife, however, cannot seek a legitimate union with Joseph.

In making her request known to Joseph, Potiphar's wife speaks directly and curtly. "Lie with me" (39:7), she insists. By using this abbreviated speech, the narrator suggests that the woman's passion is intense and lustful. Joseph's refusal, in contrast, is dignified and substantive.[11] He refers to all the elements of his job and his master's trust in him that the narrator first reported in the third person. Because of the narrator's earlier report, the reader knows that nothing is exaggerated and Joseph's speech appears sincere instead of self-righteous. Joseph reminds the woman that she is Potiphar's wife, acknowledging the rights of his master. Furthermore, the narrator shows that Joseph is concerned with the status of his behavior before God. He states, "How can I do this great evil and sin against God?" (39:9).[12] The narrator reports no response from the woman to Joseph's refusal. Instead, her actions belie that she is insistent in her demands. She speaks to him "every day" (39:10), but Joseph continues to refuse her.

False Accusations (Gen. 39:11-18)

The narrator has Potiphar's wife appear calculating when she seizes the opportunity to make demands on Joseph on a day when "there was not a single man from the men of the household there" (39:11). She repeats the same words she uttered earlier: "Lie with me" (39:12). This time she not only touches Joseph with her eyes. Rather, she "caught him by his garment" (39:12). The word used for "caught him" (*watitpĕśēhû*) has connotations of "arrest" or "capture alive."[13] The significance of this detail will soon become apparent.

On this occasion, Joseph does not answer the woman's words. Just as her earlier silence upon hearing Joseph's speech was followed by a description of her insistent actions, so too is Joseph's silence followed by a report of his consistent refusal. He flees out of her house. However, the narrator gives us an important detail. In his haste, "he abandoned his garment" by which she had caught him earlier, "in her hand" (39:12).[14] This detail about Joseph's garment signifies Joseph's innocence and fidelity to his master. However, the woman uses the garment to accuse him.[15] Whereas Tamar uses Judah's garment to prove her innocence, Potiphar's wife uses Joseph's garment to support her false accusation against him.

The formerly absent men of the household are now called upon to serve as witnesses to the woman's complaint. By including them in the account, the narrator indicates that the incident has now become public. There can be no quiet way of handling the charges against Joseph. The woman's words of accusation are wisely chosen because she includes all the other men as victims of Joseph's putative affront. "See," she proclaims, "he has brought *among us* a Hebrew to make a toy *of us*" (39:14).[16] The terms "Hebrew" and "to make a toy of" are well chosen since both can have negative connotations. "Hebrew" may be used to refer to a person of low social status, and "to make a toy of" or "to insult" (*leṣaḥeq*) also has connotations of sexual play.[17] Only in this context does she present her charge that Joseph attempted to lie with her. The garment serves as her witness and she displays it prominently beside her until her husband comes home. The reader already realizes that she has hostility for her husband because of her previous actions. Not only has she sought an extramarital union with his slave, but she has insulted her husband's judgment in the presence of the other men of the household. However, the narrator withholds her most insulting comment to Potiphar until she can speak to him directly.

In an arresting speech, the woman speaks to her husband in words that may be understood in two ways in the Hebrew:[18] (a) "The Hebrew servant, whom you have brought among us to insult me, came in to me" or (b) "The Hebrew servant whom you have brought among us, came in to me to insult me." The woman is able to insult her husband in two ways by these words. First, she accuses him of being responsible for Joseph's putative threat by emphasizing that Joseph was in her household because Potiphar brought him there. Second, as the meaning of the first translation shows, she suggests that her husband deliberately brought Joseph to insult her! However, she is protected in this outrageous charge by the ambiguity of her words, which can have the meaning of the second translation. In both meanings, another phrase has connotations that heighten the seriousness of her accusation. She charges that Joseph "came in to me" *(bāᵓ-ᵓēlay)*. This can refer to his coming into her house, but the phrase can also mean sexual penetration.[19] She maintains that Joseph was not successful in violating her, but her excuse is questionable. "As soon as I lifted up my voice and cried," she relates, "he left his garment with me and fled out of the house" (39:16). If there were no other men at home, why would Joseph flee, if in fact, he had attempted to attack her? The narrator precipitates the reader's contempt of the woman while she presents a case that enables her husband to believe her and necessitates his own defense of his judgment.

The Aftermath of the Accusation
(Gen. 39:19-23)

The narrator has shown that the woman has presented a powerful accusation against Joseph—one that has insulted her husband's ability to protect his household. The reader now awaits the judgment against Joseph. Other unfaithful servants in Egypt could be sentenced to death (40:22). Joseph, however, is sent to prison. The reality of the prison is underscored by the narrator's carefully chosen words, translated literally: "Joseph's master took him and put him in *prison,* the place where the king's *prisoners* were *imprisoned,* and he was there in *prison*" (39:20).[20] Joseph's subservience is emphasized by the contrast of his passivity with Potiphar's actions. Potiphar, who is appropriately identified as "Joseph's master" "took him" and "put him" into the prison. While incarcerated, God continues to favor him. Joseph was previously in charge of Potiphar's household; now he is put in charge of other prisoners.[21] Similarly, just as Potiphar was not concerned about any of the matters Joseph oversaw, so too is the prison-keeper confident while Joseph works for him. Joseph prospers in prison, recalling his earlier success in Potiphar's house.

Potiphar's wife does not appear again in the Joseph cycle of stories. Her role was to make the accusation that lands Joseph in prison. Beyond that, this stereotyped character has no additional function.

Conclusions

Joseph's imprisonment eventually leads to Pharaoh's recognition of him as a brilliant interpreter of dreams. Joseph rises to a position in Pharaoh's court that will lead to the rescue of his family, and hence the nascent Israelite people, from starvation. Just as God protected Joseph when his brothers sold him into slavery, so too do the unjust actions of Potiphar's wife actually lead to Joseph's rise to power.

Although the narrator's portrayal of Potiphar's wife is simplistic and stereotypical of the foreign woman as temptress,[22] the narrator's continuing account is not devoid of nuance. While it is true that this Egyptian woman unjustly accuses Joseph so that Potiphar, an Egyptian official, has him imprisoned, other Egyptians show kindness to Joseph and allow him to advance in the government. Although no additional Egyptian women with any development of characterization appear in Genesis, the reader does find that Joseph marries an Egyptian woman, Asenath, with whom he has two sons, Ephraim and Manasseh. It is striking that this woman is identified as "the daughter of Potiphara priest of On" (41:45). Although the narrator never makes an explicit identification between Potiphar and Potiphara, the similarity in their names prompts the question in the reader's mind and allows speculation as to whether Joseph and Potiphar were reconciled. Although the names originally might have had no connection (indeed, the occupations of the nameholders are distinct) the possibility remains. The descendants of one of the more important tribes of Israel, Ephraim, owe their origin to an Egyptian woman of priestly ancestry. Potiphar's wife may have cast a frightening pall on Joseph's early stay in Egypt, but her slanderous action causes him no lasting anguish. Rather, with Asenath, another Egyptian woman, Joseph continues to establish descendants for the covenantal people.

Conclusion

The narratives about the ancestors of Israel and others who are associated with Israel's origins yield important information about the self-understanding of the groups from whom they originate. The accounts of the beginnings of Israel provide a fertile setting for the expression of what is ideologically or theologically crucial for those who tell the story. The concerns that are priorities for the community often are expressed in terms of their beginnings. The Book of Genesis, with its accounts of the ancestors, along with others who interact with them or follow after them, reflects the theological understandings of God's relationship with the community. The men and women who first told the stories, as well as the community that continued to shape the accounts and in whose context the narrator works, reveal much about their views of God's role in their lives.

In this study of the texts that deal with the women of Genesis 12–50, I offer a reading that attempts to uncover the narrator's perspective of the role that these women played in Israel's origins. Without denying that the worldview from which the narrator came placed restrictions on women's activity, this interpretation of the accounts has shown that the women usually are portrayed respectfully and paradigmatically.

The initial infertility of Sarah, Rebekah, and Rachel illuminates God's role in the survival of the Israelites. Sarah's laughter and denial before God, Rebekah's pain in pregnancy, and Rachel's lament underscore God's capacity to respond to humans. God is seen not only as the one who is responsible for their pregnancies, but also as the one who protects the bearers of the Israelites from other threatening situations. Sarah and Rebekah are protected from any harm from Pharaoh and Abimelech when their husbands place them in danger, and Rachel ultimately escapes from her manipulative father and menacing brother-in-law. Rebekah hears God's direct message about the heir to the covenant and is shown to cleverly safeguard God's plan even at her own personal risk. Rachel and Leah, who compete with one another for Jacob's favor, nonetheless are in agreement concerning the safety and future of their families. Their actions and advice

114

to Jacob when he is challenged by Laban ensure that their people return to the land of the promise.

These narratives display a sensitivity for the fragile nature of God's promises. God chose three infertile women and one woman who was not sexually desirable to her husband to bear the children who would inherit the covenant. The unreasonableness of such a plan serves to dramatize the awe-inspiring qualities of the God of Israel. They also complement the narratives of the patriarchs, who also seem unlikely candidates for God's blessings. Abraham, who comes from a distant land; Isaac, who was destined for sacrifice; and Jacob, the second born, would not have been expected to be chosen by God. Similarly, Sarah, Rebekah, Rachel, and Leah, who are representative of the types of people who ordinarily might be dismissed by society, hold the key to Israel's survival under God's directive.

The narrative of Tamar illustrates the effects of the nascent covenant and its implications for the community. Placed in the literary setting of a time when the covenantal stipulations had not yet been given, this account addresses questions of justice. The narrator sympathetically recounts Tamar's plight and Judah's injustice to her. Questions of justice between Israel and its neighbors are also considered. The account of the difficulties between Hagar and Sarah demonstrates the community's concern about the implications that God's promises with Israel may have for foreign peoples. Although the Egyptians stand outside the covenant, the story of Hagar shows that the narrator is comfortable in showing that God responds to the slave woman. In addition, Hagar is portrayed poignantly in her suffering and ultimately is depicted as a woman of courage. The rape of Dinah and the effects of the revenge that her brothers take against the Shechemites are probed for their implications about the fairness of the attack and the relationships of the two groups of people who must live alongside each other. Another facet of Israel's relationship with foreigners is found in the accounts of the daughters of Lot and Potiphar's wife. Although the daughters of Lot are portrayed sympathetically, their father is shown to be selfish and unthinking. The daughters' progeny comes from a man who chooses to separate himself from the God of Abraham. Potiphar's wife is a caricature of woman as seductress, but this negative depiction is striking because it is limited. She is not only the temptress but also is a foreigner. She is feared not only because of her sexuality but also because of the distinct culture she represents. Any xenophobic tendencies in this narrative are balanced, however, by the success of Joseph and his marriage to the

Egyptian woman Asenath, who bears him two children who are the eponymous ancestors of the tribes of Ephraim and Manasseh.

When these narratives are viewed as a whole, the women of Genesis
are portrayed as both the childbearers of the promise and as people who
are intimately involved in the implications of the covenant. The major
characters, Sarah, Rebekah, Rachel, and Leah, are included in the larger
ancestral narratives. The narrator does not apologize for their inclusion or
attempt to justify God's activity among them. Rather, they are included in
the absence of a polemic. They are extraordinary in the same sense that
their husbands are, that is, they are unexpectedly successful and strong in
the face of difficulties, but they are not unusual because they are women.
The sad stories of Lot's daughters, of Hagar, Dinah, and Tamar, and the
deprecatory depiction of Potiphar's wife express the depth of the community's concern with relationships both within and outside the group.
Thus, the two priorities are kept in tension: the concern for the survival
of the covenantal community, and its relationships with its neighbors.

Because of the problems in dating the narratives in the Torah, it would
be difficult to assess the time period from which the narrator comes and
to posit what that particular community's perspective on women was at
any specified time. My approach in this book has not been to reconstruct
the historical period from which any narrative may have come, to identify
the historicity of the characters, nor has it been to reconstruct the layers
of tradition that may be present in any given text. Rather, the placement
of the narratives and their interrelationships support the position that at
some point in Israel's history the story of its origins was woven together
in a distinctive pattern by a narrator who wants to present a theological
perspective of God's involvement with the Israelites, to examine the relationships of individuals with each other, and to consider the consequences
of existence among various peoples. While it is true that the audience
probably knew the outcome of the story before it was told in this form,
the narrator structures the incidents to dramatize that what occurred might
well have been otherwise. The narrator does not tell an account of God's
activities with pious or powerful men. Rather, the men *and* women who
receive the covenantal blessings of God are newcomers to the land who
are threatened by outsiders, must struggle for their very survival, and
question God's designs. The narrator includes striking accounts of the
women in early Israel's existence who form an integral part of the story.

Although the perspectives cannot be dated from this study, some
conclusions about how women were perceived can be gleaned from the

Genesis narratives. It is true that women are under the authority of men. Sarah and Rebekah must dutifully obey their husbands, who take them into foreign lands. Only the men speak to foreign leaders. Lot's daughters are dependent upon their father, who determines where they live. Isaac, not Rebekah, gives the blessings to his sons. Rachel and Leah have no choice when Laban arranges their marriages to Jacob. Dinah cannot determine where she lives nor does she have any say in the revenge taken by her brothers. Tamar has no means of obtaining her rights of the levirate marriage. Nevertheless, the narrator shows that these women are not simply obedient vessels or passive participants in Israel's drama. Rebekah directs her unwitting husband into ensuring the future of her people according to God's directives. Rachel and Leah make it possible for Jacob to return to Canaan. Tamar's resourcefulness and courage enable her to bear a child and to escape Judah's death sentence. Even the stories of suffering or injustice show that women are included when the narrator probes the difficult questions of Israel's existence. The struggles of Sarah and Hagar, the origins of the sons of Lot's daughters, the disaster between Dinah's brothers and the Shechemites, and the injustice of Potiphar's wife toward Joseph address major questions concerning the relationships between the people of Israel and their neighbors. The narratives of Genesis 12–50, the account of Israel's origins, are not simply the stories of the patriarchs. Rather, the women of Genesis are seen as valuable contributors in this critical expression of Israel's self-understanding. They are valued as the mothers of a people who struggle to survive, as directors of their family's destiny, as the recipients of God's revelation, and as participants in the struggles for justice and self-identity as Israel defines itself in the context of its neighbors.

Notes

Chapter 1

Introduction

1. A sampling of important studies for biblical investigations includes Letty Russell, *The Future of Partnership* (Philadelphia: Westminster Press, 1979), especially the section on biblical views of sexuality, 86–88; Rosemary Radford Ruether, *Women-Church: Theology and Practice of Feminist Liturgical Communities* (San Francisco: Harper & Row, 1985), especially her discussions that critique patriarchy and delineate the ways in which women are excluded from covenantal expectations; Phyllis Bird, "Images of Women in the Old Testament," in Rosemary Radford Ruether, ed., *Religion and Sexism: Images of Woman in the Jewish and Christian Traditions* (New York: Simon and Schuster, 1974), 41–88; Rosalyn Lachs, *Women and Judaism* (Garden City, N.Y.: Doubleday & Co., 1980), especially the chapter titled, "Woman in the Bible," 88–118; Athalya Brenner, *The Israelite Woman: Social Role and Literary Type in the Biblical Narrative,* The Biblical Seminar (Sheffield: JSOT Press, 1985); Adela Yarbro Collins, ed., *Feminist Perspectives on Biblical Scholarship,* Society of Biblical Literature Centennial Publication, no. 10 (Chico, Calif.: Scholars Press, 1985); Gerda Lerner, *The Creation of Patriarchy,* Women and History (New York and Oxford: Oxford University Press, 1986); Phyllis Trible, *Texts of Terror: Literary-Feminist Readings of Biblical Narratives,* Overtures to Biblical Theology, no. 13 (Philadelphia: Fortress Press, 1984).

2. See, e.g., Alice L. Laffey, *An Introduction to the Old Testament: A Feminist Perspective* (Philadelphia: Fortress Press, 1988).

3. Robert Alter, *The Art of Biblical Narrative* (New York: Basic Books, 1981), 75.

4. See discussion by Meir Sternberg, *The Poetics of Biblical Narrative: Ideological Literature and the Drama of Reading,* Indiana Literary Biblical Series (Bloomington: Indiana University Press, 1985), 12, 84–85.

5. Throughout this book, translations are either my own or from the RSV. I use my own (usually literal) translations in order to emphasize a particular feature employed by the narrator. Otherwise, the RSV is retained and is indicated.

6. See Sternberg, *The Poetics of Biblical Narrative,* 235.

7. See the excellent discussions of the techniques of repetition in Sternberg, *The Poetics of Biblical Narrative,* 390–93; Alter, *The Art of Biblical Narrative,*

76–77, 96–97; and J. P. Fokkelman, "Genesis," in Robert Alter and Frank Kermode, eds., *The Literary Guide to the Bible* (Cambridge, Mass.: The Belknap Press of Harvard University, 1987), 46.

8. See Shimon Bar-Efrat, *Narrative Art in the Bible,* Bible and Literature Series, no. 17 (Sheffield: Almond Press, 1989), 132.

9. See Alter, *The Art of Biblical Narrative,* 60.

10. Sternberg, *The Poetics of Biblical Narrative,* 339.

11. This reference could also be cited as an example of a type-scene.

Chapter 2

Sarah

1. See Gen. 15:18-21 and Gen. 17:2-8.

2. Following the biblical nomenclature, the names of the ancestors are given as they are found in the texts being discussed. Abraham and Sarah are called Abram and Sarai before their names are changed by God to indicate their importance as the ancestors of Israel.

3. E. A. Speiser holds that Abraham's account that Sarah is his half-sister (Genesis 20) is part of Sarah's legitimate genealogical information. He concludes that "the ultimate purpose of biblical genealogies was to establish the superior strain of the line through which the biblical way of life was transmitted." See *Genesis,* The Anchor Bible, vol. 1 (Garden City, N.Y.: Doubleday, 1964), 93. While it is true that Sarah comes from the same ancestral land as Abraham, no other information about her background is given by the narrator. Abraham's accounting that she is his half-sister never is verified. An examination of Genesis 20 shows that Abraham's claims are suspect. See below.

4. See the discussion of Lot in chapter 3.

5. See Genesis 15 and 17.

6. Gen. 12:13, emphasis added.

7. In contrast, Susan Niditch concludes that "the language of the account suggests that Abram relates to Sarai lovingly and implies that they undertake the trick together." See *Underdogs and Tricksters: A Prelude to Biblical Folklore,* New Voices in Biblical Studies (San Francisco: Harper & Row, 1987), 57.

8. Claus Westermann, however, holds that her silence indicates she agrees. See *Genesis 12–36: A Commentary,* trans. John J. Scullion (Minneapolis: Augsburg, 1985), 163.

9. Others interpret the text to be ambiguous. See, for example, Peter Miscall, *The Workings of Old Testament Narrative,* The Society of Biblical Literature Semeia Studies (Philadelphia: Fortress Press, and Chico, Calif.: Scholars Press, 1983), 41.

10. Niditch concludes that the tone of Genesis 12 is not judgmental against Abram. See *Underdogs,* 45–49. However, I find that by placing the condemnation against Abram in the mouth of Pharaoh, the narrator highlights the contrast between the foreigner who seems better acquainted with the demands of the God of Israel than does Abram. See also Westermann, *Genesis 12–36,* 166.

11. This phrase is also found in Gen. 24:51, where Laban exasperatedly tells the servant that Rebekah may go after his attempts to keep her have failed.

12. See Gen. 16:3.

13. See Gen. 16:1, 2, 3, 5, 6, and 8. There are two words for maidservant used of Hagar, šipḥâ and ʾāmâ.

14. See, for example, Niditch, *Underdogs*, 48–49.

15. Miscall also raises the question of whether Hagar might be one of the maidservants acquired in Egypt. See *The Workings of Old Testament Narrative*, 45. He also notes an Arabic tradition that states Hagar was in fact one of the maidservants provided by Pharaoh.

16. A debate in the past concerning the interpretation of this account has focused upon whether there are extrabiblical data that come from the second millennium to support the action of a childless wife giving her servant to her husband for offspring to be born in the wife's name. For example, Speiser claims that Sarah's actions are congruent with paragraph 146 of the Code of Hammurabi wherein a priestess can elevate a slave woman to a wife of her husband, and if the slave acts arrogantly, the priestess can demote her, but not sell her. See *Genesis*, 120. However, John Van Seters argues that paragraph 146 of the Code of Hammurabi was used "to circumvent the law which prevented her [the priestess] from having natural offspring of her own. This practice was restricted to priestesses who were childless by law." Van Seters points out that other so-called parallels from the Nuzi documents of the 15th century B.C.E. and from Old Assyrian documents of the 19th century B.C.E. are written expressly for the benefit of the husband, whereas the narratives concerning Hagar and Sarai are "for the sake of the wife, in order that she may have children of her own." See *Abraham in History and Tradition* (New Haven and London: Yale University Press, 1975), 69–70. See also the discussions by Gerhard Von Rad, *Genesis: A Commentary*, The Old Testament Library, vol. 12 (Philadelphia: Westminster, 1961), 187; and by John H. Otwell, *And Sarah Laughed: The Status of Women in the Old Testament* (Philadelphia: Westminster, 1977), 102–3.

17. See also Sternberg, *The Poetics of Biblical Narrative*, 389. Compare Westermann's assessment in *Genesis 12–36*, 240, and Trible's analysis, *Texts of Terror*, 11–12.

18. See the discussion by Otwell, *And Sarah Laughed*, 102.

19. See also Job 19:7. J. Cheryl Exum understands this phrase as "an indictment of the patriarchal system, which pits women against women and challenges their intrinsic worth with patriarchal presuppositions about women's role." See " 'Mother in Israel': A Familiar Story Reconsidered," in Letty M. Russell, ed., *Feminist Interpretation of the Bible* (Philadelphia: Westminster, 1985), 77. While it is true that these women suffer from a patriarchal system, in the function of this narrative Hagar and Sarah give birth to two rival nations. Their contentiousness is more a reflection of the problems of the two nations than it is of individual women. Similarly, the rivalry among Leah and Rachel must be understood in the context of the tribal difficulties within Israel.

20. In contrast, Esther Fuchs argues that the repetition of phrases is indicative of Abram's innocence and shows that Sarai has no basis for accusing him. See "A Jewish Feminist Reading of the Hagar Stories," unpublished paper presented at

the conference "Gender, Race, and Class: Implications for Interpreting Religious Texts" (Princeton, N.J.: Princeton Theological Seminary, May 17, 1988), 4. The narrator's repetition, however, is used to confirm Sarai's perceptions.

21. See Judg. 11:27; 1 Sam. 24:13-16; Ezek. 34:20; and Ps. 82:1.

22. See Westermann, *Genesis 12–36*, 267. Robert Davidson suggests that in popular usage "Sarai" was derisive, and perhaps meant "to mock." He continues, "The change is thus from one whose name was Mockery . . . an object of scorn because of her childlessness . . . to one whose name is Princess." See *Genesis 12–50*, The Cambridge Bible Commentary (London, New York, and Melbourne: Cambridge University Press, 1979), 59–60.

23. See "The Literary Characterization of Mothers and Sexual Politics in the Hebrew Bible," in Adela Yarbro Collins, ed., *Feminist Perspectives on Biblical Scholarship*, 120.

24. This assessment differs from the conclusions of Sternberg, who holds that Abraham accepts Sarah's infertility "without a murmur against either the wife who leaves him childless or the God who promised to make a great nation of him." See *The Poetics of Biblical Narrative*, 343. His view does not take into account these actions of Abraham before God or his treatment of Sarah before Abimelech.

25. The literary features of verses 1–8 are compared with 19:1-3 in chapter 3.

26. For further discussion of the motif of God's role in conception see Mieke Bal, *Lethal Love: Feminist Literary Reading of Biblical Love Stories*, Indiana Studies in Biblical Literature (Bloomington and Indianapolis: Indiana University Press, 1987), 41.

27. George W. Coats writes that Sarah's laughter and the messengers' responses "offer a threat to the safety of the prospective mother by virtue of [God's] challenge." However, it is of Abraham whom God first demands an accounting. See *Genesis, with an Introduction to Narrative Literature*, 138.

28. For example, Davidson writes of Abraham, "The promise of a son through Sarah has been so long delayed that Abraham can only respond to the announcement with sheer incredulity which expresses itself through laughter." Yet of Sarah's laughter, he writes, "In the J tradition in 18:13, the name Isaac is linked with Sarah's laugh, not merely an incredulous but a bitter laugh, born of repeated frustration." Similarly, he writes of 18:11-12, "The fact that Sarah *laughed to herself* probably points to the pent-up bitterness in her thoughts." See *Genesis 12–50*, 60, 64. Similarly, Speiser describes Sarah as "down-to-earth to a fault, with her curiosity, her impulsiveness, and her feeble attempt at deception." See *Genesis*, 131. Von Rad says that Sarah has an "unbelieving and perhaps somewhat evil laugh," whereas "Abraham's silence is beautiful; it gives the reader time for many thoughts." See *Genesis: A Commentary*, 202–3.

29. See, for example, 1 Sam. 14:47; 2 Sam. 8:2; Isa. 15–16; Jer. 48; and Zeph. 2:8-11.

30. Naomi Steinberg argues that Abraham sees Sarah as expendable because she has no child and wants to be rid of her as a wife. However, her explanation would be more appropriate for the incident with Pharaoh (Genesis 12), because on this occasion Abraham has received the promise that Sarah would have a child. See

"Israelite Trickster, Their Analogues and Cross-Cultural Study," *Semeia* 42 (1988), 8.

31. See the discussion by J. P. Fokkelman, "Genesis," 48.

32. Past studies have argued that the questions about Sarai's sexual involvement with Pharaoh raised by Genesis 12 prompt the focus on Sarah's noninvolvement with Abimelech in Genesis 20. For example, Westermann writes that the account "is a search for answers to questions which the old narrative about Abraham raised." See *Genesis 12–36*, 319. Calum Carmichael holds that Genesis 20 is a reworked version of Genesis 12 made in order that both Sarah and Abraham appear in a better light. See *Women, Law, and the Genesis Traditions* (Edinburgh: Edinburgh University Press, 1979), 17. Recently, Niditch has challenged the conclusions of tradition-history studies. Genesis 20 and 26 are not based on Genesis 12, she argues, because the language used in the account is actually composed of formulaic expressions found throughout Scripture. See *Underdogs*, 39–40. Rather than seeing Genesis 20 as a reworking of Genesis 12, it is more helpful to think of it as a type-scene of the ancestress in danger. Both scenes are found in different contexts, and thus have distinct functions. See the discussion by Robert Alter in *The Art of Biblical Narrative*, 47–62.

33. Earlier source-critical studies have focused upon the differences in tone in the two accounts and argued that Genesis 12 comes from the J source, whereas Genesis 20 comes from the E source. For example, Von Rad writes that J "left open all the possibilities for what might have happened to Sarah with the king," whereas E "painfully excludes the thought that Sarah could have been touched by Abimelech." See *Genesis: A Commentary*, 225.

34. In earlier comparative studies with Ancient Near Eastern literature, commentators compared Abraham's statement that Sarah was his sister to extrabiblical texts that offered putative parallels. For example, Speiser compares the wife-sister motif with Hurrian practices and concludes that a woman who is both wife and sister (whether by birth or adoption) has a higher social standing and privileged status and thus Abraham presented this plan in order that he would have enhanced credentials. See *Genesis*, 93. The debate with extrabiblical records of the same time was effectively challenged by Van Seters, who concludes that the context for the wife-sister motif comes from "the customs and attitudes" that are documented in Egyptian and Phoenician texts of the first millennium and not from Nuzi documents of the second millennium. See *Abraham*, 71–76.

35. The formulaic phrase, "in the integrity of my heart," is found in 1 Kings 9:4 and Ps. 78:72, 101:2.

36. See Miscall, *The Workings of Old Testament Narrative*, 14–15.

37. See Isa. 3:12, 9:15, and Hos. 4:12.

38. Cf. Niditch, who argues that Abraham is portrayed sympathetically because he explains that Sarah is his half-sister, "at a point of genuine heart-baring." See *Underdogs*, 55. In contrast, Coats more accurately explains that "Abraham's designation of Sarah as sister leads to the crisis. It is a deceptive deed, and as a consequence, the appeal is almost comic, at least lame." See *Genesis, with an Introduction to Narrative Literature*, 150.

39. Carmichael is too speculative when he suggests that Abimelech's payment to Abraham "suggests that he had relations with her but in the belief that she was the man's sister." See *Women*, 17. On the contrary, the narrator uses the revelation of God to highlight that Abimelech is innocent.

40. See Westermann, *Genesis 12–36*, 328.

41. The use of *mĕsaḥēq* ("playing") may have sexual connotations, but there is no evidence that the narrator emphasizes them here. See the discussion by Westermann in *Genesis 12–36*, 339.

42. In light of this ambiguous phrase, it would be better to translate the following verse "*And* God said to Abraham . . .*" instead of "*But* God said to Abraham . . .*" as does the RSV.

43. In contrast, Von Rad argues that verse 12 is "the 'tense moment' in the structure of the narrative, for the reader has not expected that God would be on Sarah's side, but rather on Abraham's." See *Genesis: A Commentary*, 228. Von Rad makes two assumptions. Although the narrator is sympathetic to Hagar's plight, the narrator recognizes that Sarah's predicament is difficult as well. Moreover, the narrator does not portray Abraham's motivations and sympathies simplistically.

44. In discussing the portrayals of Sarah and Hagar, Athalya Brenner suggests that "their chief aim in life is to become biological mothers . . . Sarah does not feel secure until she gets rid of her inferior rival altogether. The implication is that women cannot cooperate even when they share a common purpose." However, if it is remembered that Ishmael and Isaac represent two contentious nations, it can be seen that it is not accurate for the narrative to be given personal connotations about women in general. See *The Israelite Woman*, 93.

45. It is also true, however, that Moses's father-in-law was from Midian and that the Midianites assisted Israel in the wilderness (Num. 10:29-32).

46. For the references to the deaths of the patriarchs see Gen. 25:7, 35:28, and 47:28. Sarah lives longer than Moses, who dies at 120 (Deut. 34:7).

Chapter 3

The Daughters of Lot

1. In Hebrew, *malāk* (angel) is always masculine.

2. See my earlier study, "The Characterization of Lot in Genesis," *BTB* 18 (1988), 123–29.

3. See, for example, L. Heyler, "The Separation of Abraham and Lot: Its Significance in the Patriarchal Narrative," *JSOT* 26 (1983), 85. I do not agree with his assessment that Lot was previously considered by Abram as heir. Although Genesis 15 is the first reference to Eliezer as heir, this does not necessarily imply that it is only at this time that Abram chose him. In fact, in Abram's conversation with God, the impression is that Eliezer had been heir for a period of time. Moreover, the references to Eliezer are not presented in such a way to link this choice of Abraham to any frustration over his relationship with Lot.

4. See the discussion of the promise of land by W. Vogels in "Lot, père des incroyants," *Eglise et Theologie* 6 (1975), 139–51. Vogels also argues that Abraham

offered the land because he was weaker than the younger Lot and was trying to avoid a conflict he knew he could not win. See Vogels, "Lot in His Honor Restored: A Structural Analysis of Genesis 13:2-18," *Eglise et Theologie* 10 (1979), 5–12. However, the placement of Genesis 14 after the problems encountered by Abram with Lot concerning the land heightens the impact of Abram's rescue of Lot. It is Abram who is stronger.

5. Umberto Cassuto points out that this verse recalls Gen. 2:6. Both texts are "classic examples of a land blessed with fertility." The reader knows, moreover, that the land would have remained fertile if humans had not sinned. See *A Commentary on the Book of Genesis, Part One: From Adam to Noah* (Jerusalem: Hebrew University, 1961), 104, 117.

6. It is interesting to note that Rashi states that the reason Lot was captured by the kings of the east (14:12) was precisely because he chose to dwell in Sodom. See A. M. Silbermann, ed., *Pentateuch with Rashi's Commentary* (London: Shapiro Vallentine, 1945), 56.

7. God changes Abram's and Sarai's names as a sign of the promise of progeny. See the discussion in chapter 2.

8. Bruce Vawter holds that Lot's response to the men in 19:1 is "modeled on the reaction ascribed to Abraham in 18:2-5. It already carries with it an implied rebuke of the boorish ways of the rest of the men of Sodom." See *On Genesis: A New Reading* (Garden City, N.Y.: Doubleday, 1977), 232. It is true that the meeting of Lot with the angels deliberately recalls Abraham's meeting with them, but it is crucial to note the differences between the two meetings before judgment is rendered concerning any evaluation. The narrator is not so much contrasting Lot's treatment of the angels with that of the townspeople as in pointing out the difference between Abram's and Lot's response to the messengers of God and to the divine plan. This is clear from the similar language and setting of the respective texts.

9. T. D. Alexander notes the similarities in the opening scenes of Abraham's and Lot's encounters with the men and concludes that the "almost identical ways" in which Abraham and Lot are presented show that "since Abram is commended for his generosity Lot is therefore also to be viewed in a favorable light." See, "Lot's Hospitality: A Clue to His Righteousness," *JBL* 104 (1985), 290. I argue, however, that the differences are deliberate and crucial for understanding the narrator's intent.

10. The rabbis conclude that Lot has less of a religious outlook than does Abraham. The Midrash records that Abraham was careful to ask the angels to wash first and then stay with him in contrast to Lot who first offered them to stay. They comment that the meaning of this is that "Abraham was particular about the pollution of idolatry, whereas Lot had no objection to it." *Gen. Rab.* 50:4. While it is clear that the text does not mention Lot's idolatry, the rabbis accurately note that the text makes this comparison in order to contrast Lot's behavior with Abraham's.

11. *On Genesis,* 235–36.

12. John Skinner, *A Critical and Exegetical Commentary on Genesis,* The International Critical Commentary, vol. 1, 2nd ed. (Edinburgh: T. and T. Clark, 1930), 307.

13. Gerda Lerner, *The Creation of Patriarchy,* Women and History (New York and Oxford: Oxford University Press, 1986), 173.

14. Ibid., 175.

15. Ibid., 172.

16. Susan Niditch correctly points out that the potential rape of the divine messenger is "a doubly potent symbol of acultural, non-civilized behavior from the Israelite point of view." It is also important to note that the threat of sexual brutality to the daughters would also be reprehensible in Israelite perspective. See "The 'Sodomite' Theme in Judges 19–20: Family, Community, and Social Disintegration," *CBQ* 44 (1982), 369.

17. See the excellent introductory discussion of hospitality by Bruce J. Malina in "Hospitality," Paul J. Achtemeier, ed., *Harper's Bible Dictionary* (San Francisco: Harper & Row, 1985), 408–9.

18. In contrast, George W. Coats reads the closing of the door as a way to defend the guests. See "Lot: A Foil in the Abraham Saga," in J. T. Butler et al., eds., *Understanding the Word: Essays in Honor of Bernhard W. Anderson, JSOTS* 37 (Sheffield: JSOT Press, 1985), 121.

19. Rabbinic tradition suggests that Lot had four daughters—two who would be the virgin daughters, and two who were married to Lot's sons-in-law. See *Gen. Rab.* 50:9.

20. Gerhard Von Rad suggests that the sons-in-law "were so unable to receive the message that it seemed ridiculous to them." The text, however, is ambiguous on this point. See *Genesis: A Commentary,* 214.

21. The etymology of "Lot" is obscure. Nonetheless, the audience would have heard the play on words. See Skinner, *A Critical and Exegetical Commentary on Genesis,* 236.

22. See *On Genesis,* 242.

23. Coats argues that the daughters and Lot are the sole survivors of the catastrophe and were stranded in the cave. However, the way this independent tradition has now been woven into the completed text heightens the action of Lot who chose to settle in the cave whereas the angels allowed him to go to Zoar. See "Lot: A Foil in the Abraham Saga," 125.

24. Of this reference Josephus concludes, "There, isolated from mankind and in lack of food, he passed a miserable existence," although Josephus still places Lot in Zoar. Overall, however, Josephus interprets Lot in a positive light. *Ant.* I: 204.

25. Skinner presumes that verse 31 "presupposes a universal catastrophe in which the whole human race had perished, except Lot and his two daughters." See *A Critical and Exegetical Commentary on Genesis,* 314. There is nothing in the text that could support this view. Similarly, R. Davidson argues that the daughters thought that "they were the sole survivors of catastrophe," and thus are commended for their actions to perpetuate humanity. See *Genesis 12–50,* 78. I agree that the daughters are not explicitly condemned and that there are extenuating circumstances that place their actions in a sympathetic light, but these circumstances

are the isolated locality to which their father has deliberately brought them and his failure to provide them with husbands.

26. See, for example, Gen. 23:19; Judg. 6:2; Isa. 2:19; 1 Sam. 24:4; 1 Kings 19:13; and Ezek. 33:27.

27. Skinner argues, "The intoxication of Lot shows that the revolting nature of the proposal was felt by the Hebrew conscience." See *A Critical Exegetical Commentary on Genesis*, 313. While it is true that the judgment is against the incestuous union, I think the narrator wants the reader to understand Lot's severe intoxication as an additional indication of his irresponsibility.

28. The clearest indications that rabbinic tradition regards Lot negatively are found in the statements of the rabbinic assessment of the incestuous union. For example, *Gen. Rab.* 51:9 records, "R. Nahman b. Hanin observed: Whoever is aflame with adulterous desire is eventually fed with his own flesh. R. Judah of Gallia and R. Samuel b. Nahman both said in the name of R. Elijah Enene: We would not know whether Lot lusted after his daughters or they lusted after him but that it says, He that separateth himself seeketh desire (Prov. XVIII, 1) whence it follows that Lot desired his daughters."

Chapter 4

Hagar

1. See above, chapter 2.

2. See earlier discussion in chapter 2.

3. To be more precise, the name Hagar *(hāgār)* comes from the root *hgr*, whose meaning is unknown, although it appears to be related to an Arabic cognate that means "forsake, retire." The word *haggēr* comes from the root *gwr*, meaning "sojourn." However, to the readers of this narrative, the words sound similar and related. See Francis Brown, S. R. Driver, and Charles A. Briggs, *A Hebrew and English Lexicon of the Old Testament* (Oxford: Clarendon, 1953; reprint 1977), 157–58, 212.

4. The word *'iššâ* can refer to wife or concubine, as does the Akkadian cognate *aššatum*. See the explanation by E. A. Speiser, *Genesis*, 117.

5. See the discussion of Sarai's actions in chapter 2. Gerhard Von Rad is correct in seeing the giving of a wife's slave to the husband as accepted practice, but incorrectly concludes that this custom is viewed by the narrator with "great delinquency." See *Genesis: A Commentary*, 186. It is the specific problem with Hagar and Sarai, and not the custom per se that is being commented upon. Cf. Cynthia Gordon's comments in "Hagar: A Throw-Away Character Among the Matriarchs?", SBL Seminar Papers No. 24 (1985), 273.

6. It is appropriate to note the general assessment of the status of women in such situations by Gerda Lerner. She writes that first or primary wives, concubines, and slaves all are "under sexual dominance and regulation, but the degree of their unfreedom varies by class . . . the married wife is at one end of the spectrum, the slave woman at the other, the concubine in an intermediate position." See *The Creation of Patriarchy*, 112.

7. In contrast, Esther Fuchs concludes that Abram's silence is an indicator of the narrator's negative characterization of Sarai because she alone instigated the rivalry between her and Hagar. See "A Jewish Feminist Reading of the Hagar Stories," 2–3.

8. Phyllis Trible rejects the translation of "contempt" or "disdain" for *qll*, and prefers "lowered in esteem." See *Texts of Terror*, 12. See also my discussion in chapter 2.

9. John H. Otwell goes too far when he compares Hagar's action to paragraphs 146 and 147 of the Code of Hammurabi and suggests that "Hagar had acted as if her pregnancy had made her a free woman. Sarai asked Abram to confirm Hagar's legal standing." There is no specification of the legality of Hagar's feelings. See *And Sarah Laughed*, 103.

10. Gordon argues that Hagar is the only woman who receives direct revelation from God. She discounts the apparent statement of God to Sarah in Genesis 18, because the text is ambiguous and may be indicating that Abraham, and not God, is speaking to Sarah. She also discounts the communication with Rebekah, calling it indirect. See "Hagar," 276. I disagree with these assessments. The context of the encounter with Sarah does indicate a communication with God, and Rebekah is indeed addressed directly concerning the twins in her womb.

11. For the use and omission of Hagar's name when encountering the angel, see Trible, *Texts of Terror*, 14–15.

12. Cf. Trible, *Texts of Terror*, 16–17.

13. As George W. Coats appropriately remarks, the angel's announcement to Hagar concerning Ishmael's destiny "does not, however, constitute a resolution of the tension between Hagar and Sarai; it relates directly to the son." See *Genesis, with an Introduction to Narrative Literature*, 131.

14. See Hos. 8:9; Jer. 2:24; and Job 24:5.

15. John Van Seters appropriately points out that although Hagar must return to submit to Sarai, she "is given the knowledge that the son to be born to her will have a destiny that will be anything but submissive and his defiance will be her ultimate vindication." See *Abraham*, 193.

16. It is interesting to note that although the narrator specifies that the angel of God appears to Hagar, Hagar responds that this visit is tantamount to a visit by the Deity itself. Some interpreters have explained such responses as an indication that the original narrative specified that God does in fact appear to Hagar, and that this was later changed to the messenger to avoid the theological problem of having God appear to a human being. However, the narrative may also be original in its present form. Hagar has the experience of the angel, but recognizes God's presence in that experience. See the excellent discussion by Claus Westermann in *Genesis 12–36*, 242–44.

17. See the discussion in chapter 2.

18. See the discussion in chapter 2.

19. See especially the detailed analysis of the opening verses, Gen. 21:1–13.

20. Other studies in comparing this account with that in Genesis 16 make assessments concerning which narrative is original. Van Seters, for example, sees

Genesis 21 as an example of "a case of a literary composition variant of the earlier story with direct knowledge and dependence on it." For his assessment of the arguments that Genesis 21 "is an individual variant of chapter 16," see *Abraham*, 198–202. For similar arguments, see Speiser, *Genesis*, 156–157, Von Rad, *Genesis: A Commentary*, 186, 230. For a comparison of similar literary features between Genesis 16 and 21, see Robert C. Culley, *Studies in the Structure of Hebrew Narrative* (Philadelphia: Fortress, and Missoula, Mont.: Scholars Press, 1976), 43–46. I find the conclusions of Robert Alter to be most convincing. Instead of seeing Genesis 21 as dependent on Genesis 16 and as a revision of it, he sees the similarities and repetitions as "dependent on the manipulation of a fixed constellation of predetermined motifs." See *The Art of Biblical Narrative*, 51.

21. See Isa. 47:15, 53:6; Job 38:41; Ps. 119:176, and especially Ps. 107:4.

22. The word *śiaḥ*, meaning "complaint," is found in Job 7:13, 9:27, 10:1, 21:4, and 23:2. The word *śiaḥ*, meaning "bush," is used in only three other places in the Bible: Gen. 2:5; Job 30:4, 7.

23. See Trible, *Texts of Terror*, 25–26.

24. What Lerner says of Mesopotamian women is appropriate in this situation as well: "Patriarchal society featured patrilineal descent, property laws guaranteeing the inheritance rights of sons, male dominance in property and sexual relations, military, political, and religious bureaucracies." See *The Creation of Patriarchy*, 106.

25. See Gen. 34:18, 37:2, 43:8, 44:22; 1 Sam. 2:12, 16:11; 2 Sam. 18:5, 12; 1 Kings 3:7.

26. Cf. the explanation by Trible in *Texts of Terror*, 25–26. Although Ishmael's name is never used by Sarah, Abraham, God, or the narrator in Genesis 21, this should not in itself be used to argue that his personhood is lessened, for even Hagar refers to him as "the child" (21:16).

Chapter 5

Rebekah

1. Meir Sternberg presents a different assessment. He argues that Rebekah's name is obscured since it is found in the middle of the genealogy, and that Maacah is presented more prominently. However, the narrator clearly indicates that Maacah is born of a concubine, an indication of her lower status. See *The Poetics of Biblical Narrative*, 133.

2. Recent studies on Genesis 24 have included source-critical, form-critical, and tradition-history investigations. George W. Coats argues that the entirety of chapter 24 comes from the J source and that it is most likely that "J did not create the story but rather adapted it for his purposes from an oral source." See *Genesis: with an Introduction to Narrative Literature*, 169–70. John Van Seters similarly concludes that "chap. 24 is a unified literary work" of the J author "with no indication of any dependence upon a folkloristic tradition of Isaac as a forefather of Israel." See *Abraham*, 248. In his discussion of source-critical studies, Van Seters investigates some of the reasons other researchers have used to posit more

than one source but concludes that with some rearranging, one can reconstruct a "better narrative flow" (see p. 240). John Skinner sees various doublets and repetitions and concludes that chapter 24 is a combination of two earlier narratives. See *A Critical and Exegetical Commentary on Genesis*, 340. Instead of restructuring the text, I attempt to investigate the purposes these repetitions or peculiar ordering serve in the final edition of the narrative. Claus Westermann's form-critical investigation argues that the account was originally a family narrative but was reworked "into a guidance narrative" to stress God's assistance. See *Genesis 12–36*, 383–84. Wolfgang M. W. Roth's tradition-critical study of chapter 24 argues that the setting of the text is "the last will and testament of the patriarch Abraham" and that it becomes the J author's "interpretative epilogue of his Abraham cycle." See "The Wooing of Rebekah: A Tradition-Critical Study of Genesis 24," *Catholic Biblical Quarterly* 34 (1972), 177, 179. An excellent narrative-critical study of chapter 24 can be found in Sternberg, *The Poetics of Biblical Narrative*, 131–52. This chapter is based on my earlier study, "Images of Rebekah: From Modern Interpretations to Biblical Portrayal," *BR* 34 (1989), 33–52.

3. The intention of the account of Sarah's death and burial, on one level, is to show that Abraham legally bought the cave of Machpelah from the Hittites. On another level, however, the placement of this chapter in the context of the Isaac and Rebekah cycle serves as a transition.

4. While acknowledging that the genealogy of chapter 22 sets the stage for the introduction of Rebekah in chapter 24, Roth does not find that the information found in chapter 23 is similarly significant for understanding chapter 24. However, surely the account of the death of Sarah prompts the reader to consider the next generation. See "The Wooing of Rebekah," 177.

5. Cf. Gen. 18:11; Josh. 13:1, 23:1,2; 1 Kings 1:1.

6. Of this oath, E. A. Speiser states, "Since sons are said to issue from their father's thigh . . . an oath that involved touching this vital part might entail the threat of sterility for the offender or the extinction of his offspring." See *Genesis*, 178.

7. Roth and Coats posit that an earlier form of this story focused upon the servant and his role, enabling it to be used as an example story for other servants and ambassadors. Below, I discuss the ambiguities of the account that cast doubt on the appropriateness of the servant's actions and thus I disagree that he would be held up as a model. See Roth, "The Wooing of Rebekah," 180–81, and Coats, *Genesis, with an Introduction to Narrative Literature*, 170.

8. In his unit on "Oral Transmission and Biblical Texts," Robert C. Culley compares and contrasts three scenes that occur "at the well" and eventually lead to marriage. See *Studies in the Structure of Hebrew Narrative*, 43. See also Westermann, *Genesis 12–36*, 382.

9. Josephus writes that Rebekah was the only woman of several who gave him water. *Antiquties* I: 242–49.

10. See the discussion by Sternberg, *The Poetics of Biblical Narrative*, 134. Since the possibilities are numerous, it is all the more significant that the woman whom the servant meets is indeed from Abraham's family and is of marriageable age and status.

11. See discussion by Sternberg, *The Poetics of Biblical Narrative*, 138–40.

12. The translation of *mištā²ēh* in the RSV, "gazed at," does not fully capture the connotation of the Hebrew text. Although the hithpael from *š²h* may be translated "gaze," presuming that the root *š²h* is a variant of *š<ᶜh*, this more likely comes from the root *š²h* ("make a crash"). See Brown, Driver, and Briggs, *A Hebrew and English Lexicon of the Old Testament*, 980–81.

13. See Gen. 34:5; Exod. 14:14; Judg. 18:19; 2 Sam. 13:20, 19:11; 2 Kings 18:36; Jer. 4:19; et al.

14. In contrast, Westermann argues that there is no tension except to wonder "whether God grants success or not" to the servant. See *Genesis 12–36*, 382. Van Seters is correct when he comments that the lack of difficulty underscores God's "hidden assistance," yet his comment that "it is this lack of any difficulty that completely negates the dramatic storytelling interest of the whole episode" does not recognize the crescendo of ambiguity in the account. See *Abraham*, 243. Similarly, Speiser's estimation that the narrator "relate[s] in unhurried detail how Rebekah was found and won" belies the tension in the text. See *Genesis*, 182.

15. Westermann argues that the giving of gifts to Rebekah "is nothing other than his joyful reaction to the girl's obliging readiness to refresh him and the animals (not some sort of bride price!); his unbounded joy is reflected in the presents . . ." (*Genesis 12–36*, 387). It is impossible to assess whether the concept of an "official" bride price is appropriate here, but it is clear that the narrator does not use this incident merely to express the servant's joy. The gifts were given to the servant by Abraham to go to the woman who would accompany the servant on the return journey. See also the discussion by Skinner in *A Critical and Exegetical Commentary on Genesis*, 344. Robert Alter provides a careful reading of this account, but I disagree with his conclusion that only after the servant is certain of Rebekah's family background does he present the jewelry. See *The Art of Biblical Narrative*, 53. Cf. Westermann who states that it is only after the servant presents the gifts that he "inquires about the girl's family and accommodation in her house." See *Genesis 12–36*, 387.

16. The Hebrew reads: *wayyiqah hā²îš nezem zāhāb beqaᶜ mišqālô ûšěnê šěmîdîm ᶜal-yādêhā ᶜăśārâ zāhāb mišqālām.*

17. Some of the versions noted these difficulties. The Samaritan Pentateuch adds *wayyāśem al ²appāh* (which he placed upon her nose) and Pseudo Jonathan adds *yhb* after *ᶜl ydh²* (which he placed upon her arms).

18. The use of *badderek* (24:27) recalls the use of *darkô* in 24:21 and reinforces the viewpoint that the journey was successful only at this point.

19. Sternberg does not judge her response to be an actual offering of hospitality. However, her comment clearly implies that the servant and the camels will indeed be accepted. Moreover, his judgment that "protocol forbids the girl's inviting him herself," is presumed, not proven. See *The Poetics of Biblical Narrative*, 142–43.

20. Cf. 24:20.

21. Some commentators have noted that Rebekah's household is referred to both as her "father's house" (24:23) and as her "mother's house" (24:28). Van Seters rightly points out that these need not lead to the conclusion that two sources must

be posited, because the first phrase is used by the servant who is asking a question, and the second phrase would customarily be used by a daughter speaking of her home. See *Abraham,* 240.

22. Van Seters' comment, namely, "The long repetition in the servant's speech, from vv. 34–49, is certainly anticlimactic" misunderstands the narrator's intention. See *Abraham,* 244. Similarly, in discussion of the servant's speech, no account of the discrepancies with what actually happened is considered by Westermann in *Genesis 12–36,* 388.

23. Sternberg correctly notes that the servant says this to show that "he would not commit himself as long as there remained the slightest doubt about the alignment of human wishes with divine disposition." See *The Poetics of Biblical Narrative,* 151.

24. Speiser's comment that "the servant himself gains in stature with each phase of the story" does not take into account this evidence. See *Genesis,* 184.

25. The versions attest to the ambiguity of this phrase. Targum Onkelos reads *ᶜdn bᶜdn ᵓô ᶜśrh,* a time in time (i.e., a year) or ten months. This reading agrees with the interpretation found in *T.B. Ket.* 57b that understands *yāmîm* as "a year." See Moses Aberbach and Bernard Grossfeld, eds., *Targum Onkelos to Genesis* (Center for Judaic Studies, University of Denver: Ktav, 1982), 144–45.

26. Roth correctly points out that Rebekah follows Abraham's example of obedience since her reply recalls his response to go willingly to a foreign land. He further points out that various key words link them. They both leave behind "their country," "their kindred," and "their father's house." Both will be "blessed" and "become great." See "The Wooing of Rebekah," 178–79. James G. Williams appropriately underscores the significance when he says, "With this blessing the narrator quietly moves Rebecca into the cycle of God's promises to the patriarchs." See *Women Recounted: Narrative Thinking and the God of Israel,* Bible and Literature Series, vol. 6 (Sheffield: Almond Press, 1982), 44. See also Mary Donovan Turner, "Rebekah: Ancestor of Faith," *Lexington Theological Quarterly* 20 (1985), 42–50.

27. Van Seters argues, in contrast, that Rebekah's comment in 24:57 is only in response to whether she is ready to leave immediately. However, this ignores the content of the narrative. Until this point, many contingencies could have kept Rebekah from leaving with the servant and she was free to decide to stay. See *Abraham,* 240.

28. Van Seters argues that the presence of both "nurse" and "maidens" does not necessarily point to two sources, and concludes "the reference to the 'nurse' must certainly be suspect, for Rebekah scarcely has need of a wet nurse . . . until she has infants." On the contrary, the reference to the nurse helps us to anticipate the children she will bear. See *Abraham,* 241.

29. Skinner contends that the original reading referred to Isaac being comforted after the death of his father and that "the change would naturally suggest itself after J's account of the death of Abraham had been suppressed in accordance with P's chronology." See *A Critical and Exegetical Commentary on Genesis,* 348–49. However, as has been shown above, the introduction of Rebekah in chapter 24 follows the information that Sarah has died, as was given in chapter 23.

30. The account does note, however, that Isaac was forty when he married Rebekah, but sixty when the twins were born (25:20, 26).

31. The Hebrew reads: ʾim-kēn lāmmâ zeh ʾānōkî "if it is thus, why is it that . . ." Targum Onkelos reads: ʾm kn lmh dnn ʾnʾ, "if so, what do I need this for?" See Moses Aberbach and Bernard Grossfeld, eds., *Targum Onkelos to Genesis*, 150–51. The Syriac adds the equivalent of ḥayyâ, hence the RSV translation, "if it is thus, why do I live?"

32. See, for example, Christine Garside Allen, "Who Was Rebekah? 'On Me Be the Curse, My Son!' " in Rita M. Gross, ed., *Beyond Androcentrism: New Essays on Women and Religion*, American Academy of Religion Aids for the Study of Religion, no. 6 (Missoula, Mont.: Scholars Press, 1977), 200, 204.

33. John Goldingay explores this theme and notes that both Abraham and Isaac father two nations. See "The Patriarchs in Scripture and History," in A. R. Millard and D. J. Wiseman, eds., *Essays on the Patriarchal Narratives* (Winona Lake, Ind.: Eisenbrauns, 1980), 7.

34. tām may be translated "of integrity, sound, wholesome," and not simply "quiet." It comes from the root tmm, meaning "to be complete or finished." See Brown, Driver, and Briggs, *A Hebrew and English Lexicon of the Old Testament*, 1070–71.

35. Coats is correct in recognizing that verse 28 provides "a foreshadowing" for the account of the blessing of Jacob in chapter 27. However, this is incomplete without recognizing that the oracle itself is proleptic of the entirety of the Jacob and Esau cycle. See "Strife without Reconciliation: a Narrative Theme in the Jacob Traditions," *Werden und Wirken des Alten Testaments: Festschrift für Claus Westermann zum 70. Geburtstag* (Göttingen: Vandenhoeck und Ruprecht, and Neukirchen-Vluyn: Neukirchener Verlag, 1980), 98.

36. See Alter's penetrating analysis in *The Art of Biblical Narrative*, 42–46.

37. For allusions and contrasts, see David L. Petersen, "A Thrice-Told Tale: Genre, Theme, and Motif," *BR* 18 (1973), 41. For an examination of the putative parallels with the Nuzi documents and "Hurrian" law see Thomas L. Thompson, *The Historicity of the Patriarchal Narratives: The Quest for the Historical Abraham*, Beiheft zur Zeitschrift für die altestamentliche Wissenschaft, vol. 133 (Berlin and New York: Walter de Gruyter, 1974), 234–48.

38. The accounts of Abraham and Sarah were related before Sarah had children, and thus were told to show that God protected them, and thereby, the promise was assured. It may be posited that this text was originally told as an event that occurred before Isaac and Rebekah had children. Robert Polzin stresses the additional theme of the interconnectedness of progeny and wealth. See " 'The Ancestress of Israel in Danger' in Danger," *Semeia* 3 (1975), 81–98.

39. Petersen correctly identifies the theme of "patriarchal success in a foreign context" but incorrectly emphasizes this theme to the exclusion of others. He states, "The emphasis is not on Isaac's relationship to Rebekah or Isaac's relationship to the king." See "A Thrice-Told Tale," 42. Yet clearly the speech patterns show that these relationships are crucial.

40. Westermann holds that Rebekah is operating from a particular perspective that the right of the firstborn, in the case of twins, seems unfair and that "the

mother objects to this exclusive prerogative of the one son. Revolt against a 'social' injustice lies behind her plan." See *Genesis 12–36*, 438.

41. Coats sees verse 5a as a transition scene that reveals how Rebekah learned of the plan of Isaac, "But at the same time, it highlights the tension in the relationship between Rebekah and Isaac. Rebekah was not privileged to the conversation between Isaac and Esau—the address is explicitly from Isaac to Esau; yet she heard." See *Genesis, with an Introduction to Narrative Literature*, 201. Skinner writes, "The clever but heartless strategem by which Rebekah succeeds . . . is related with great vivacity and with an indifference to moral considerations." See *A Critical and Exegetical Commentary on Genesis*, 368. See also Turner, who states, "We are left in ambiguity" concerning Rebekah's motivation, in "Rebekah: Ancestor of Faith," 46.

42. While this story may originally have circulated without the context of the birth oracle, it cannot be ignored in its current structure.

43. See Gen. 18:9-15.

44. Skinner correctly points out that Jacob's objection "throw[s] his mother's resourcefulness into bolder relief." See *A Critical and Exegetical Commentary on Genesis*, 370.

45. See "Who Is Hiding the Truth? Deceptive Women and Biblical Androcentrism," in Adela Yarbro Collins, ed., *Feminist Perspectives on Biblical Scholarship*, 137–44.

46. Allen, "Who Was Rebekah?," 184; and Turner, "Rebekah: Ancestor of Faith," 42.

Chapter 6

Rachel and Leah

1. See the discussion in chapter 7.

2. Claus Westermann comments that this first description of Rachel shows that "at that period girls helped with the work and were able to move among the men freely and unhindered and without the veil." While this statement exaggerates women's freedom, it is true that Rachel is shown to be somewhat independent in her work as a shepherd. See *Genesis 12–36*, 465.

3. Robert Alter suggests that the stone is a symbol of Rachel's blocked fertility and that this symbol serves as a reminder of other events in Jacob's life where stones feature prominently. See *The Art of Biblical Narrative*, 55.

4. See, for example, Prov. 1:17 and Mal. 1:10.

5. For discussion of the description of Leah's eyes, see Speiser, *Genesis*, 225. The word can also be translated as "tender." Whether her eyes have the negative connotations of weak or the positive of tender, the narrator clearly is contrasting Leah's ordinary appearance with Rachel's extraordinary one.

6. Gerda Lerner argues that this narrative indicates the early practice of matrilocal marriage (which gave the women more autonomy and divorce rights). When Rachel later steals Laban's gods, Lerner argues, an example of the patrilocal marriage superseding matrilocal marriage is seen. It is difficult, however, to use

this single narrative (with its emphasis on the deceptive practices of Laban and the cunning of Jacob and Rachel) to posit any historical information about the original preference of matrilocal marriages. See *The Creation of Patriarchy,* 167–68. Concerning the issue of a "bride-price," Gerhard Von Rad writes, "Even though one cannot speak expressly of a 'bought marriage' in Israel, still it was the common notion that daughters were a possession, an item of property that could be transferred from one owner to the other without further ado." See *Genesis: A Commentary,* 285. Similarly, Westermann writes that Jacob is not offering a purchase price per se, but that the narrative contains "the widespread motif in tale and story where the suitor . . . must produce some worthy achievement to win the bride." See *Genesis 12–36,* 467. Some scholars have argued that Jacob's work is tantamount to a son-in-law adoption marriage, but see the convincing arguments against such hypotheses by John Van Seters in *Abraham,* 78–82.

7. See Gen. 24:67 and 34:3.

8. Zvi Jagendorf points out that it is Leah who actually knows Jacob and that Jacob knows Leah "*as Rachel,* for the image in his mind prevails over the presence of the woman at his side." See " 'In the Morning, Behold, It Was Leah': Genesis and the Reversal of Sexual Knowledge," *Prooftexts* 41 (1984), 189–90. George W. Coats points out that the word used to describe the feast, *mišteh,* derives from the root meaning "drink." Coats suggests that Jacob was too drunk to notice that his bride was Leah. See *Genesis: with an Introduction to Narrative Literature,* 214.

9. See the discussion by Susan Niditch, *Underdogs,* 107.

10. 2 Sam. 13:15; Deut. 22:13, 16, 24:3.

11. Deut. 21:15-17.

12. The emphasis is often a polemical one against the Canaanite gods Baal and Anat.

13. Gen. 15:2; Jer. 22:30; Lev. 20:20, 21.

14. Deut. 7:14; Exod. 23:26; Gen. 11:30, 25:21; Judg. 13:2, 3; 1 Sam. 2:5; Job 24:21; Ps. 113:9; Isa. 54:1.

15. See Mary Callaway, *Sing O Barren One: A Study in Comparative Midrash,* Society of Biblical Literature Dissertation Series, no. 91 (Atlanta: Scholars Press, 1986), 28.

16. For a discussion of the interpretive, improvised derivations of the names of the sons of Jacob and the significance for the tribal system, see Von Rad, *Genesis: A Commentary,* 290–91.

17. Gen. 37:11.

18. Alter emphasizes that "the brusqueness of this is even a little more emphatic in the Hebrew where give, '*havah*,' is a word often used for peremptory and crudely material requests . . . and where the tense of dying is more imminent (literally, 'I am dead')." See *The Art of Biblical Narrative,* 187.

19. Cf. Alter who concludes that she is "impatient, impulsive, and explosive." Ibid., 187.

20. Niditch appropriately comments that Jacob's retort to Rachel's lament betrays "perhaps, his own disappointment and bitterness." See *Underdogs,* 97.

21. Esther Fuchs argues that Rachel's exclamation appears childish and that the reader would sympathize with Jacob's response. I argue, in contrast, that the narrator chooses Rachel's language for its dramatic effect. See "The Literary Characterization of Mothers and Sexual Politics in The Hebrew Bible," in Adela Yarbro Collins, ed., *Feminist Perspectives on Biblical Scholarship,* 123. Cf. Westermann, *Genesis 12–36,* 474.

22. The lack of recorded controversy concerning the use of Bilhah and Zilpah as surrogate mothers may indicate that this was an accepted practice. It appears clear, however, that the children retain their identities as offspring of their biological mothers. The narrator refers to Leah's children, Issachar and Zebulun, as the fifth and sixth sons, whereas if Zilpah's children, Gad and Asher, were counted equally as the children of Leah, Issachar and Zebulun should be reckoned as the seventh and eighth sons. Moreover, when Jacob gathers his wives and children to meet Esau, he separates the children to remain with their own mothers. The children of Zilpah and Bilhah remain with them. See also the listing of Jacob's sons in Gen. 35:22–26.

23. See the discussion by Callaway, *Sing,* 26.

24. See Prov. 31:29; Song of Sol. 2:2, 6:9; Isa. 32:9; Dan. 11:17.

25. See the discussion by Athalya Brenner, *The Israelite Woman,* 94. Brenner argues that "Jacob's love is sought after not for its own sake, but as a means for begetting more male heirs." One must not forget, however, Leah's desperation for Jacob's love.

26. Gen. 30:14, 15*bis,* 16.

27. Niditch shows that this scene reveals the "association of women with the power of the household." See *Underdogs,* 98.

28. That daughters were less highly esteemed is clearly apparent in this narrative. The narrator does not quote Leah's naming of Dinah, nor does the narrator give the significance of her name. Leah does not connect the birth of Dinah with any potential for community esteem or the respect of her husband.

29. See the use of this word in Isa. 4:1 and 54:4.

30. Mieke Bal, *Lethal Love,* 84–85.

31. See the discussion by Westermann, *Genesis 12–36,* 477, and Niditch, *Underdogs,* 97.

32. Fuchs argues that the narrator presents women as wanting to fulfill patriarchal expectations and thus legitimizing patriarchal ideology, and that personal fulfillment is not at issue. I argue, however, that both issues are supported in these narratives. See "The Literary Characterization," 128–29.

33. God's command to Jeremiah not to have a wife or children is not an exception because it is prompted by the punishment of the Exile.

34. This is numbered as the first of the 613 mitzvoth in Jewish tradition.

35. See the discussion by Callaway, *Sing,* 32.

36. Westermann, *Genesis 12–36,* 490–93.

37. 1 Kings 11:1, 8; Ezra 10:2, 10, 11, 14, 17, 18, 44; Neh. 13:26, 27; Cf. Prov. 2:16.

38. Fuchs argues that Rachel and Leah condemn their father because of "vindictiveness as they stress their economic deprivation by their father," but that Jacob does not sound bitter because he stresses God's intervention while discussing his plans with his wives. This comparison is not complete, however, since Jacob's response to Laban upon the completion of Laban's search of the tents is a powerful condemnation based upon Jacob's long-term economic deprivation. See "'For I Have the Way of Women': Deception, Gender, and Ideology in Biblical Narrative," *Semeia* 42 (1988), 72.

39. See the discussion by Westermann, *Genesis 12–36*, 490–93.

40. Earlier studies suggested that Rachel's theft of Laban's gods was a way to secure Jacob's right of inheritance to Laban's estate. See Speiser, *Genesis,* 250. As Moshe Greenberg has shown, however, possession of household gods was not an indicator of who had right to the estate; moreover, a written document was necessary to clarify the ambiguity of ownership. See "Another Look at Rachel's Theft of the Teraphim," *JBL* 81 (1962), 239–48, and the discussion by Van Seters, *Abraham,* 93–94.

41. See also Deut. 28:29.

42. Significantly, Laban now "searches" the tent; he no longer "feels about" (31:35). When Jacob later confronts Laban, he says that although he has searched through everything, he has not found the gods (31:37). If, of course, Laban was in fact able to *feel* everything, he would have found them.

43. Fuchs argues that the Bible ignores the necessity of women who must act deceptively because they are powerless in a patriarchal society. Far from ignoring the link between powerlessness and deception, the narrator clearly portrays it in this scene where Rachel, who is threatened both by Laban's accusations and Jacob's unwitting sentence of death, protects herself against both men without soliciting anyone's help. See Fuchs, "Who Is Hiding the Truth? Deceptive Women and Biblical Androcentrism," in Adela Yarbro Collins, ed., *Feminist Perspectives on Biblical Scholarship,* 140.

44. Fuchs also argues that the narrator shows Rachel to be acting in a morally ambiguous manner because her motivation for taking the gods is not specified and her expression of "the way of women" could refer to menstruation or to the act of deception itself. See "For I Have the Way of Women," 68–83. However, the narrative context shows that the motivation is clear: it is revenge against the father. In addition, the ambiguity regarding whether or not she is menstruating simply serves to underscore that this condition of a woman cannot be verified by a man without his becoming ritually impure in the process. See Naomi Steinberg, "Israelite Tricksters, Their Analogues and Cross-Cultural Study," *Semeia* 42 (1988), 7–9; and Mieke Bal, "Tricky Thematics," *Semeia* 42 (1988), 151–52. Steinberg correctly concludes: "That the trickster appears often and with impunity suggests that this role was a form of power available to those who lacked other means to achieve their goals," 8.

45. See Fuchs, "Deception, Gender, and Ideology," 76.

46. Coats emphasizes that the scene definitively demonstrates Laban's downfall. See *Genesis, with an Introduction to Narrative Literature,* 220.

47. Von Rad correctly sees parallels between this account and other stories of the foolishness of idols, such as in Judg. 17 and Isa. 44:9-20. See his discussion in *Genesis: A Commentary*, 305. See also Westermann, *Genesis 12-36*, 495.

48. The word *ʾiššâ*, used of Bilhah and Zilpah (Gen. 30:4, 9), is sometimes translated "concubine," although the more common word for concubine is *pilegeš*. The word *ʾiššâ* is most frequently translated as "woman."

49. Coats aptly remarks that previously "Rachel's desire for a child consumes her life. Here her delivery represents her death." See *Genesis, with an Introduction to Narrative Literature*, 240.

50. Cf. Fuchs, "The Literary Characterization," 132-33.

51. Leah is mentioned by Jacob one more time. While in Egypt, he gives instructions to his sons concerning his death, insisting on burial with his ancestors at Machpelah. In listing the names of his ancestors, he refers to his having buried Leah there. The emphasis is not so much on the fact that he wants to be buried with Leah, as it is on the importance of being interred in his own land with his forebears. See Gen. 49:29-33.

Chapter 7

Dinah

1. Here the term "Israelite" is used to refer to one of the descendants of Jacob, also known as Israel.

2. The name of Dinah also appears in Gen. 30:21, where she is identified as being the daughter born to Leah and Jacob.

3. For the additional importance of this story for understanding various laws in Deuteronomy, see Calum M. Carmichael, *Women, Law, and the Genesis Traditions*, 33-48.

4. Dana Nolan Fewell and David M. Gunn, "Tipping the Balance: Sternberg's Reader and the Rape of Dinah," unpublished paper presented at the Society of Biblical Literature Annual Meeting (Chicago, Ill.: Nov. 20, 1988).

5. Mishael Maswari Caspi, "'And His Soul Clave Unto Dinah' (Gen. 34)— The Story of the Rape of Dinah, the Narrator and the Reader," *Annual of the Japanese Biblical Institute* 11 (1985), 16-53.

6. As Frank Moore Cross points out, the terms "Hivite," "Amorite," and "Hittite" are all used in the sense of "Canaanite"; all designate the "original inhabitants of the 'land of Canaan.'" See *Canaanite Myth and Hebrew Epic: Essays in the History of the Religion of Israel* (Cambridge, Mass., and London: Harvard University Press, 1973), 46.

7. See Gen. 33:1-17 and 35:1-8. In contrast, George W. Coats argues that "the story remains isolated in its context." See *Genesis, with an Introduction to Narrative Literature*, 234. Similarly, Michael Fishbane states that Genesis 34 is distinct within the Jacob cycle and serves as an interlude. See "Composition and Structure in the Jacob Cycle (Gen. 25:19—35:22)," *JJS* 26 (1975), 15-38; and *Text and Texture: Close Readings of Selected Biblical Texts* (New York: Schocken Books, 1979), 40-62.

8. The Hebrew text reads, *wayĕhabĕqēhû*. The suggested emendation of *BHS*, *wayyēbk* (and he wept) does not have any textual support; rather, it presumes that the subject of the verb must be the same as the subject in the previous verbs found in verse 4.

9. Although the present is unspecified in 33:10-11, a previous reference details the bounty of animals gathered to be presented to Esau. See Gen. 32:13-21.

10. The Hebrew verb that "returned" is translating is *yšb*, which might also be translated, "was enthroned" or "reigned." Indeed, the conflict between Esau and Jacob is a political one.

11. The narrator does not relate whether Esau discovered Jacob's deception. Esau's role disappears after this report.

12. The Hebrew word is *šālēm*.

13. Stuart A. West assumes that Jacob allowed Dinah to go out alone and that this permissive attitude contributed to the wrong done to her. See "The Rape of Dinah and the Conquest of Shechem," *Dor le Dor* 7 (1980), 144. However, the narrator does not mention Jacob in this context, nor does West address Dinah's decision.

14. The Hebrew reads, *wayyiqqaḥ ʾotâ wayyiškab ʾōtâ wayĕʿannehā*. The word *wayĕʿannehā* is usually translated "humbled," but this does not fully capture the meaning of the cruel act.

15. Meir Sternberg comments that the narrator "first shocks us by the suddenness of the rape and only then proceeds to its aftereffects on the rapist." See his detailed analysis of Genesis 34 in *The Poetics of Biblical Narrative*, 441–81.

16. See Sternberg, *The Poetics of Biblical Narrative*, 447.

17. The phrase "he spoke the heart," *yĕdabēr ʿal lēb*, implies not only tenderness and kindness, but may imply that he asked Dinah's forgiveness as well. See especially Gen. 50:21. See also the discussion by Phyllis Trible in *Texts of Terror*, 67.

18. Current scholarship is divided on how to judge Jacob. Carmichael states that Jacob "proceeds in a practical, expedient manner," since this "man of experience [is] not so beset by physical desires and hence [is] not so bothered by them." See *Women*, 35. Robert Davidson argues that Jacob has a minor role and comments on the pragmatic aspects of the plan. See *Genesis 12–50*, 197. It is more accurate, however, to see both motives in tension.

19. E. A. Speiser correctly comments that the "spotlight rests throughout on the next generation." See *Genesis*, 266. It is important to note, however, that Jacob's "minor part" is a deliberate narrative technique that highlights this contrast between the two generations.

20. The Hebrew reads: *ûbĕnê yaʿăqob bāʾû min-haśśādeh kĕšāmʿām wayyitʿaṣṣĕbû hāʾănāšîm wayyiḥar lāhem mĕʾōd*. See the discussion by Sternberg, *The Poetics of Biblical Narrative*, 451–52.

21. Speiser, in contrast, argues that Hamor is "peace-loving and conciliatory." It is true that his tone is not argumentative, but by avoiding what happened to Dinah, it is hard to conclude that he is truly a man of peace. See *Genesis*, 268.

22. Claus Westermann suggests that the final version of the Dinah account incorporates the polemic against intermarriage found in Deuteronomy 7 and comes from the exilic period. See *Genesis 12–36*, 544–45. It is clear that during the early settlement (conquest), the Israelites whose roots were as slaves in Egypt and various socioeconomic groups of Canaanites became one people, and it should be expected that intermarriage occurred regularly.

23. Davidson correctly underscores the abuse of the sacred sign of circumcision by the sons, because they use it to incapacitate the men and strip it of its true significance. Moreover, he states, the Hivites see it merely as the price to pay for an increase in economic strength. See *Genesis 12–50*, 196.

24. See the discussion by West, "The Rape of Dinah and the Conquest of Shechem," 147.

25. Historical-critical analyses of this text would suggest that the account is an example of an entire group of local Canaanites who joined the *apiru* revolt. Perhaps it contains echoes of a dissenting group from the Exodus contingent who believed that local Canaanites were joining too easily without fully understanding what it meant to acknowledge YHWH as God. Norman Gottwald states that the narrative "may indeed carry us back into a historico-social setting in which either a small group of proto-Israelites or a larger assemblage of Israelite tribes was considering a modus vivendi with Shechem which was to include intermarriage." See *The Tribes of Yahweh: A Sociology of the Religion of Liberated Israel, 1250–1050 B.C.E.* (Maryknoll, N.Y.: Orbis, 1979), 311. Cf. A. de Pury, "Genese XXXIV et l'histoire," *RB* 71 (1969), 5–49.

26. Speiser argues that "Simeon and Levi are all but condemned for their primitive impulses." See *Genesis*, 267. Carmichael concludes that the author sides with them, and that "the concern of Simeon and Levi with their sister's honor recalls the strict sexual morality of the wisdom literature of Joseph in regard to Potiphar's wife (a wisdom narrative), and of Deuteronomy." See *Women, Law, and The Genesis Tradition*, 33–35. Sternberg suggests that the identity of Simeon and Levi as Dinah's full brothers increases our sympathies for their actions. See *The Poetics of Biblical Narrative*, 468–69. John Otwell argues that "this may reflect a legal obligation not reported in the law codes" or may underscore their "particular affection." See *And Sarah Laughed*, 115. I see the identification more as a means to explain their particular interest in the revenge.

27. West is too speculative in his suggestion that originally Simeon and Levi proposed the circumcision as a tactic only to free their sister. See "The Rape of Dinah and the Conquest of Shechem," 151.

28. Sternberg states that Dinah was detained in Shechem's house, but the text never addresses the issue of Dinah's feelings or whether she remained willingly. See *The Poetics of Biblical Narrative*, 456. See also West, "The Rape of Dinah and the Conquest of Shechem," 145, 149.

29. Deut. 22:28-29. See also 2 Sam. 13:15-19.

30. This same expression is used also by the psalmist who describes how God protected Israel "when they were few in number" (Ps. 105:12 = 1 Chron. 16:19 RSV). The phrase points to the overwhelming odds suffered by Israel. Sternberg,

in contrast, sees his comment to be one of cowardice and immorality. See *The Poetics of Biblical Narrative*, 448,473.

31. Westermann points out that when Simeon and Levi do not accept Jacob's rebuke they "show a break not only between two generations but between two epochs." See *Genesis 12–36*, 544.

32. See also Exod. 23:27 and Josh. 10:10.

Chapter 8

Tamar

1. The thematic connections and literary features that link the story of Judah and Tamar with the Joseph cycle are debated. Calum Carmichael stresses the wisdom character of Genesis 38 and concludes that Judah's youthful experience with Joseph determines his future. See *Women, Law, and the Genesis Traditions*, 57–72. Gary Rendsburg views both Genesis 38 and Genesis 49 as connecting interludes in the Joseph cycle. See *The Redaction of Genesis* (Winona Lake, Ind.: Eisenbrauns, 1986), 83–86. Robert Alter interprets the word and thematic connections that link the accounts and concludes that both stories show "the reversal of the iron law of primogeniture." See *The Art of Biblical Narrative*, 6–10. George W. Coats, however, concludes that such linkages ultimately are "superficial," and that "this story is completely isolated from the Joseph story." See *Genesis: with an Introduction to Narrative Literature*, 273. As this discussion shows, however, the narrative must be examined in its context.

2. See, for example, Exod. 23:2; 1 Sam. 8:3; Judg. 9:3; and 1 Kings 2:28.

3. Adullam was a Canaanite stronghold that Joshua eventually defeated. See Josh. 12:15.

4. Although the final version of this account was written at a time when a negative judgment was cast on Canaanite behavior, the roots of this account show that Canaanites and Israelites readily intermarried. Norman Gottwald suggests that both Judah and Hirah represent leaders of their communities and the ensuing contacts between their people. See *The Tribes of Yahweh*, 561–62. I disagree with Claus Westermann's assessment that the present form of the text finds "no embarrass-ment" in Judah's association with Canaanites. See *Genesis 37–50: A Commentary*, trans. John J. Scullion (Minneapolis: Augsburg, 1986), 51. Clearly Judah's dis-tancing from his brothers and his association with the "Adullamite" encouraged his untrustworthy behavior in the view of the narrator.

5. For an assessment of the variants associated with the reading *wĕhāyâ bikĕzîb*, see J. A. Emerton, "Some Problems in Gen. 38," *VT* 25 (1975), 339–41. There are no other references to Chezib in the Bible, but similar names appear in Josh. 15:44, Mic. 1:14, and 1 Chron. 4:22.

6. See the discussion by J. A. Emerton, "An Examination of a Recent Struc-turalist Interpretation of Genesis XXXVIII," *VT* 26 (1976), 90–91.

7. The *hiphil* of *mwt* is used of God as a penalty for severe wrongdoing, such as in Gen. 18:25; Exod. 4:24; Num. 14:15; Deut. 9:28, 32:39; Judg. 13:23; 1 Sam. 2:6, 2:25, 5:10,11; 2 Kings 5:7; Isa. 65:15; Hos. 9:16; 1 Chron. 2:3, 10:14.

8. For discussion on the original meaning of the root *YBM*, see Miller Burrows, "The Ancient Oriental Background of Hebrew Levirate Marriage," *BASOR* 77 (1940).

9. Modern interpreters are divided on the meaning of the levirate obligations. For example, Eryl Davies argues that the widow would continue to have the brother-in-law's support whether or not she had a child who could inherit the dead husband's property. See "Inheritance Rights and the Hebrew Levirate Marriage (Gen. 38)," *VT* 31 (1981), 138–44. Coats, however, argues that marriage was not required since Judah does not specifically tell Onan to marry Tamar, and since Judah himself does not marry her. See "Widow's Rights: A Crux in the Structure of Genesis 38," *CBQ* 34 (1972), 274. Yet, as Davies points out, this is an argument from silence. Moreover, Gen. 38:14 specifically says that Shelah had not been given to Tamar "in marriage." See also Deut. 25:1-10, where it is stated that the brother-in-law not only has sexual relations with the widow, but marries her.

10. See, for example, Gen. 6:17, 9:15; Exod. 21:26; 2 Sam. 1:14; and Jer. 12:10.

11. As Susan Niditch explains, Tamar, a young childless widow, is in a particularly difficult situation and Judah's desire to have her return to her father's house "appears highly irregular. She no longer belongs there." See "The Wronged Woman Righted: An Analysis of Gen. 38," *HrvTR* 72 (1979), 146.

12. Sometimes the story of Tobit is offered as providing a parallel (see Tob. 3:7 and 8:9), but the stories are distinct.

13. As Niditch explains, there were functioning harlots who lived outside the categories of the virginal daughter or the child-bearing wife. Tamar's action at first appears ordinary. See "The Wronged Woman Righted," 147. Similarly, Athalya Brenner argues that association with prostitutes "is not forbidden but, because of the social stigma involved, is better carried out discreetly." See *The Israelite Woman*, 82.

14. For a discussion of the importance of the types of clothing that Tamar wears, see Nelly Furman, "His Story Versus Her Story: Male Genealogy and Female Strategy in the Jacob Cycle," in Adela Yarbro Collins, ed., *Feminist Perspectives on Biblical Scholarship*, 111–12.

15. See the discussion by Brenner, *The Israelite Woman*, 78–83, and Westermann, *Genesis 37–50*, 54.

16. Other commentators see the usage of *zōnâ* and *qĕdēšâ* to be interchangeable, but this opinion does not take into account the different speakers of the narrative. See, for example, John H. Otwell, *And Sarah Laughed*, 159.

17. In contrast, Westermann argues that Judah's search for Tamar is the narrator's attempt to portray him as "an honorable man." This assessment does not sufficiently consider Judah's discussion with Hirah. See *Genesis 37–50*, 54.

18. Westermann states that Judah has the right to pass sentence on Tamar as a matter of family law. While the account does not question his authority, the narrator never specifies that his actions were in the purview of acceptable custom or law. See Westermann, *Genesis 37–50*, 54.

19. Michael Astour goes beyond the evidence of the story when he argues that Judah's decree of punishment shows that Tamar was considered a member of the

cult personnel. See "Tamar the Hierodule: An Essay in the Method of Vestigial Motifs," *JBL* 85 (1966), 194.

Chapter 9

Potiphar's Wife

1. Nelly Furman argues that the actions of both women express their "resentment and rebellion." She continues, "Their interference breaks up the exclusive father-son dialog and forces recognition of their presence." See "His Story Versus Her Story," 114.

2. The importance of the relationship between the two texts was noticed by Rashi. However, he concluded that Potiphar's wife was supposed to be interpreted as being as righteous as Tamar. According to his conclusions, Potiphar's wife knew she was to be related to Joseph's offspring, but she was not certain whether she was to be their mother or was to be related through her daugher, whom Rashi equates with the daughter of Potiphara. See *Pentateuch with Rashi's Commentary*, 190.

3. See the discussion above, chapter 8.

4. Cf. the analysis by Mieke Bal in *Lethal Love*, 95–96.

5. The term *sārîs* is used of Potiphar in 37:36 and 39:1. The Midrash interprets the meaning as eunuch, arguing that Potiphar intended to use Joseph for sodomy. See *Gen. Rab.* 86:3.

6. Gen. 41:45, 50; 46:20.

7. The Midrash (*Gen. Rab.* 83:3) equates them, as does Rashi. See *Pentateuch with Rashi's Commentary*, 204.

8. See Claus Westermann, *Genesis 37–50*, 61.

9. Interestingly, the Midrash says that the bread refers to his wife. See *Gen. Rab.* 86:6.

10. Gen. 12:11 and 29:17.

11. Robert Alter comments similarly. See *The Art of Biblical Narrative*, 73, 109.

12. George W. Coats argues that the references to God "play no crucial role in the scene," and that Joseph acts only out of his sense of responsibility to his master. Coats makes a distinction between Joseph's "reason" and his "refusal." This distinction is not convincing because the narrator shows no dichotomy between his thoughts and words. See *Genesis, with an Introduction to Narrative Literature*, 279.

13. See Josh. 8:23; 1 Sam. 15:8; and 1 Kings 20:18.

14. Other occasions of the presence of significant garments in Joseph's life are recalled by this reference: the coat his father gave him, the linen he receives when he is recognized by Pharaoh, the clothing he gives his brothers, and the garment he rends in mourning. See Furman, "His Story Versus Her Story," 109–10.

15. Ibid., 108–9.

16. Emphasis added.

17. For the use of "Hebrew" in Genesis, see Gen. 39:14, 17, 41:12, 40:15, 43:32. But contrast Gen. 14:13. For "to make a toy of," see Gen. 26:8.

18. See Robert Alter, *The Art of Biblical Narrative*, 110, and Rashi, *Pentateuch with Rashi's Commentary*, 192–93.

19. Cf. Gen. 6:4, 16:2, 30:3, 38:8, 9.

20. Emphasis added.

21. See Alter's presentation and his analysis of the repetition of themes and words throughout the Joseph cycle. He points out, for example, that while in jail, Joseph is in another "pit," recalling his incarceration by his brothers. At the same time, he is in a "jail house," echoing the earlier emphasis that Joseph was in his master's "house." See *The Art of Biblical Narrative*, 111–12.

22. See Athalya Brenner, *The Israelite Woman*, 111–12, 121.

Scripture Index